T0146580

TRENZAS ~ BRAIDS

Voces de Inmigrantes de Resiliencia y Esperanza
Immigrant Voices of Resiliency and Hope

Jorge Dante Hernández Prósperi

authorHOUSE®

AuthorHouse™
1663 Liberty Drive
Bloomington, IN 47403
www.authorhouse.com
Phone: 1 (800) 839-8640

Artists Acknowledgement

Original cover drawing by Mark Oberfest "Trenzas"
Mark lives in Chappaqua, New York with his wife and two children.
He developed an interest in creating art into a lifelong passion.
Mark works with many different mediums including charcoal, graphite and oil.
The author is grateful to Mark for designing the book's cover.
See more of Mark's artwork on Instagram: @obsart123Inside
~

Inside book drawing by Dr. Sofya Helena Asfaw "The Last Pose"
Sofya lives in Cleveland, Ohio and is a Trauma Surgery and
Surgical Critical Care Physician.
Aside from her successful medical career, she is a
talented artist who shared with us her rendering
of the "Last Pose"
~

Thanks to Ashley Averill of Hite Photo, West Bloomfield, MI
for providing knowledge and guidance on digital formatting.

Published by AuthorHouse 09/05/2017

ISBN: 978-1-5462-0497-8 (sc)
ISBN: 978-1-5462-0496-1 (e)

Library of Congress Control Number: 2017912803

Dedicatoria

A mis antepasados/as, padres, esposa, hija y nietos.

~

Dedication

To my ancestors, parents, wife, daughter and grandchildren.

CONTENTS

ACKNOWLEDGEMENTS

This book reflects a collaboration with many friends and scholars who over the past 17 years invested their valuable time, effort and guidance in me. First, I thank Dr. Karen Tonso, lead dissertation advisor, who provided the academic rigor, provocative classroom knowledge, appreciation for qualitative research methods, professionalism and mentoring that enabled each of her students to respect the integrity of the doctoral process. I am but one of many doctoral students grateful for her conscientiousness and selfless dedication to have doctoral students take pride in their work, find their voice, attain self-empowerment and continue to extend the discourse on democracy, social justice and equality.

My sincere thanks to the doctoral committee members, Dr. José Cuello, Monte Piliawsky, Dr. Marc Rosa and to the late Dr. Otto Feinstein for being supportive instructors who from 2000-2007 provided valuable classroom experiences, indispensable references and contacts with the Latino/a community and the Detroit School District. I am also grateful to Dr. Jorge L. Chinea, Director of the Center for Latino/a and Latin American Studies at Wayne State University and to Dr. José Cuello, who ably directed the former Center for Chicano-Boricua Studies. It was an honor to work with these two dedicated crusaders who continue to lead, teach, mentor, protect and improve the lives of Latino/a students on a daily basis.

My admiration and gratitude to the scholar, author and expert on Latino/a Critical Theory Dr. Gerardo López who from a distance inspired and encouraged me to pursue the research study in order to continue the work through qualitative critical research of Mexican immigrant families and the schooling of their children.

Thanks to Dr. Carolyn Mears for her innovative contributions to Poetics for capturing voice and representing story. Her research provided the pivotal methodological insights that allowed me to empower the participants in my study to tell their stories in their own voices.

Invaluable to the study and the emergence of the Poetics were the Mexican parents who volunteered willingly to participate in extensive interviews over seven years, candidly sharing their childhood experiences in Mexico, their parental perceptions of education, their personal stories regarding opportunities to attend school or not, their perceptions of parental involvement and their dedication and love for their children.

OVERVIEWS

Jorge Chinea, PhD
The LatinX Perspective

Carolyn L. Mears, PhD
The Gateway Approach Paradigm

Beverley Geltner, PhD
Advocacy and Agency

Trenzas: Weaving a Tapestry of Diasporic LatinX Self-Affirmation

Jorge Chinea

As I read Trenzas I began reflecting about literacy in Latin America and the Caribbean, where the effective ability to read and write was, and continues to be, available to a privileged few. During Iberian colonial times the marginalized residents of what was then dubbed the New World were excluded from the vernacular of the dominant personas de calidad, that is, from the language of the lettered elite. The Europeans who controlled the means of production and presided over the colonial social order primarily wanted the labor of the Amerindians, enslaved African captives and all the other lower-class nonwhite castas. Generally deprived of access to formal reading and writing skills, the exploited workers preserved much of their experiences orally in songs, legends, rituals, rumors, jokes, gossip, innuendo, doublespeak, metaphors, and other forms of popular expression. In a word, they created, nurtured and sustained novel ways to validate their worldviews amidst a Eurocentric and classist environment intent on silencing, ostracizing, negating and erasing their agency.

After the former colonies became the modern-day states of the region, a restructured oligarchy of landowners, merchants, creditors and self-serving caudillos (strongmen) seized power over the liberated territories. As a result, new groups of materially impoverished people emerged to fill the changing laboring needs of the rural and urban enclaves, such as llaneros, gauchos, peasants, artisans and domestic workers. Not unlike their predecessors in the colonial era, they too received few of the social rewards available in the modernizing nations in which they lived. When their ability to eke out a living reached a breaking point, they reluctantly picked up whatever worldly possessions they had and migrated in search of better opportunities, both internally within the region and externally, primarily to the industrializing metropoles of Europe and the United States. Although the new American and European patronos (bosses) welcomed their hands—thus the term braceros or manual workers given to many of them—the newcomers sought to preserve their full humanity by passing on their personal stories of uprootedness, displacement, resettlement, and survival to friends and relatives, in a continual process "de generación a generación" (from one generation to another).

In fact, we owe some of the more iconic works of LatinX literature to pioneering emplumados and emplumadas who transformed these oral traditions into written narratives. As Ethnic and Cultural Studies scholars have rightfully observed, much of their literary production can be read as autobiography or as cultural ethnographies. By poring over such classic poems, short stories and novels as Yo Soy Joaquín, Bless Me Última, Down these Mean Streets, Working in the Dark, House on Mango Street, El Bronx Remembered, Dominoes and other Stories, Y No Se lo Tragó la Tierra and Barrio Boy, to name a few, the reader is immersed in the authors' personal journey. Conceptually, Trenzas falls squarely within this artistic genre. Methodologically, however, the work significantly enhances this body of literature by creatively contextualizing the sub-texts expressed by working-class Mexican immigrants that are often missed, minimized, ignored or lost in translation.

Hernández Prósperi re-examines their interviews, which were initially designed to elicit information on the barriers driving the systemic miseducation of their children, to delve deeper into the expressive symbols, imagery and other cues that shed light on the class, ethnic and racial discrimination they faced almost daily in their adopted new homes. For many parents who had not yet mastered English, the language hurdles prevented them from being properly heard, and hence from conveying their feelings and from seeking remedies to their victimization. The author rescues their muted voices and allows them to speak on their own terms, revealing a wealth of new information, glimpses of their inner world that seldom make it to the mainstream literary canon.

In addition, he places these revelations in perspective by re-examining his family's own transplantation from Argentina to the United States, a journey that was not devoid of many of the same challenges that other newcomers also confront. By doing so, the author does not explicitly seek to draw parallels and contrasts between the Mexican and Argentinean migratory and resettlement experiences in el Norte. Rather, he stresses the larger human picture by accentuating the role played by Latin American values in cushioning their transition to North American life. These values, of course, are contoured by the uniqueness of culture as it evolved in Mesoamerica and the Southern Cone, respectively. However, amidst this diversity Hernández Prósperi finds commonalities, including self-respect, determination, love, familism, parenthood, resiliency and an unrepressed desire for self-improvement (ganas). But he also uncovers, and lays bare, the painful legacy of colonialism in shaping notions of race and class that mutated into today's cultural wars, white privilege, ethnic separatism, and exploitative laboring conditions.

In short, Trenzas weaves the quotidian struggles of "las otras vidas," of those other lives often left out of the canonical narratives, into an engaging, bilingual work of poetic justice. By using trenzas (braids) as a mnemonic devise, Hernández Prósperi interlaces his interlocutors' responses, which become testimonials, in order to knit a collective portrait of the interviewees and the world around them. The result is a literary quilt that reveals threads of self-reliance, of not giving up, of standing tall and of starting anew in a sometimes foreign land in spite of chronic poverty and the persistence of ethnic, racial and class-based exclusion, discrimination and oppression.

The Gateway Approach Paradigm

"We know the world through the stories that are told about it."
Denzin & Lincoln, 2005, p. 641

Carolyn Lunsford Mears

The stories we hear as children shape our awareness of the world. Our parents tell us of their past; playmates regale us with funny stories of siblings and tales of hateful injustices from rivals. As we grow older, recollections from friends, family, and colleagues bring us information, guidance, joy, sorrow, and much that we learn as we grow to adulthood. When we listen to the evening news, we comprehend an event more clearly if we hear stories of the individuals affected instead of the general tally of numbers of people involved. Through stories, we put a face on statistics, and numbers become humanized.

These narratives enrich our lives with meaning and help shape our interactions with others. However, a different kind of knowledge, more potent and transformative, can be experienced when we are privileged to hear or read narratives collected through in-depth research interviews.

For those who seek to shed light on unseen margins of human experience, in-depth interviews can build connections across boundaries of awareness. A candid and ethical sharing can develop resonant understanding of how events and circumstances are experienced by others on a deeply human level. From that, we can learn about the human experience and how to make things better for those who need support and service.

I first entered the realm of narrative inquiry after deciding to research the effects of the Columbine shootings on the parents and families of students who survived the tragedy. I knew from my own experience the hardship and devastation the tragedy wrought on families, for I am a Columbine mom.

My younger son, a sophomore at Columbine High School in 1999, survived the tragedy. My family and indeed the entire community saw first-hand how abruptly and inexplicably lives were altered that day. A few quick moments of violence stole lives, shattered dreams, and re-shaped futures. The effects of the tragedy are ongoing.

Living the trauma and witnessing the hardship and sorrow that such violation brings, I wanted to do something to help those who might find themselves in a similar situation in the future. I enrolled in a doctoral program at the University of Denver to conduct research and find ways of helping survivors and their families reclaim their lives and move toward wholeness in the aftermath. My research involved extensive, in-depth interviewing, producing volumes of wonderfully informative transcriptions—over 600, single-spaced pages of stories, each rich in significance and meaning.

I was in awe at the gift the participants had given me, stories of deep pain and resilience, injury and recovery, sadness and humor, all freely shared for the purpose of benefitting others. I knew I could not do justice to the reality of the experience by attempting to re-tell their

3

stories through summary or interpretation. These stories deserved to be told in the words of the speaker and presented in their totality, yet the sheer magnitude of "data" made that impossible.

As a result, I decided to share the narratives by distilling them to their essence, eliminating the unnecessary words and transitions, condensing the experiences into the barest yet most powerful words, stepping aside and connecting the reader with the speakers directly by sharing their actual expressions. I wanted their voices to be heard, not mine, and instead of telling about what happened, I wanted to share it, evoking a resonance of understanding on a deeply human level. What remained when extraneous words were removed appeared as a poetic narrative, intense, provocative, impossible to ignore.

When I had completed my research, I was surprised at the interest other researchers expressed in my approach to investigating from the "inside" of an experience. I was encouraged to share the approach with others and at the urging of the American Educational Research Association wrote a book explaining the process I had used, Interviewing for Education and Social Science Research: The Gateway Approach.

In the process of sharing my approach, I was introduced by a colleague to Jorge Prósperi. He was working on his dissertation at the time, looking for a way to share the richness of his own research. As he read my Columbine study, he found a process that aligned with his own goals for sharing his remarkable research. His dissertation is masterful, with poetic representations that are both moving and revealing, pointing the way to the need for empathy, intervention and better educational planning.

I was pleased that he found utility in my approach, and now, years later, am deeply honored to be asked to contribute a commentary to Trenzas, a truly exemplary text. I must note, however, that a text so pure and inspiring hardly needs comment.

To read the poetic narratives that Dr. Prósperi has crafted for Trenzas is to be forever changed. The soul-baring honesty and compassionate distillation of humanity encountered herein shatters any sense of complacency or presumption of understanding how others live. Through exquisite interweavings of language and love, poems reveal the core life experiences of people who are otherwise beyond the margins of the known, often living concealed from the majority by nature of their status and origins.

As you begin to read this beautiful volume, be prepared to experience the exquisite pain of discovery, for you may find your assumptions about others will be challenged. The rawness will stay with you, and touch your heart and your thinking, especially if you work with immigrant children and families. Without a doubt, Trenzas should be required reading for every teacher, administrator, social worker, and indeed everyone who cares to learn about life as it is lived.

The poems in *Trenzas* are a gift. Savor each one . . . and remember.

"Thou Shalt Not Stand Idly By"

Beverley Geltner

My own experiences as a child of immigrants left indelible impressions that shaped my forty-year career as a high school teacher, counselor, principal, school district administrator, professor and educational researcher.

On the one hand was the awareness of my good fortune, permanently embedded in my consciousness. Barely a day passed that my parents did not express their gratitude on being safe with their young child in a new land, while across the sea their homeland and their families were being exterminated by madmen. They discovered the blessings of a democratic society where hope was reborn, support was rendered, and citizenship ultimately earned. As I progressed through the stages of early childhood, I soon found myself preparing for school—real school where the "big kids" went, and where I would meet new children, have fun playing with them, and learn to read and write. Hiding the details of the distant horrors that were engulfing my forever-to-be unknown relatives, they rejoiced in the wonderful opportunities that school afforded me. Free quality public education started for me in kindergarten and ultimately led to a Ph.D. in Educational Leadership from the esteemed University of Michigan.

I never forgot the early years of my schooling, for while I was given extraordinary opportunities that forever changed my life, I retained the memories of being from another place, of being among others who did not share my background, culture or history, of being the official linguistic translator and social liaison between my teachers and my parents. It was not until years later that I recalled at both an intellectual and emotional level what it meant to be "other" and how the experiences of that reality shaped me, from my first day in kindergarten through my decades-long career.

We were immigrants: they were "other"; we were Jewish: they were other; we celebrated our holy days: they celebrated theirs; we were few: they were many; our parents did not finish elementary school: theirs were professionals; my parents advised silence and keeping one's head down; theirs advised speaking up, heads held high…as if…as if it were their natural right to have a voice and be heard.

I was a good student and rejoiced in my parents' pride at my growing success. Over time, I gained access to hallowed, unimaginable centers of learning and scholarship. As my career unfolded, I found myself in the position of professor, charged with the responsibility of preparing future educational leaders with knowledge, wisdom, and an unwavering moral compass.

"You must take a stand," I would urge them. "You must be clear about what it means to be an educational leader and why you intend to take on this onerous task." I warned them, "You will be pressured from all sides by true believers who will challenge you. Your decisions will not always be supported. They will try to silence you. They will want you to honor their loud voices, their privileges, their history. "But remember," I urged them, "to be an educational leader is to think deeply and wisely about what your mission is, whom you serve, and where you stand." "You will be challenged; you may even be vilified when you make public your commitment to all, and your dedication to welcome all, embrace all, and assume responsibility for their futures."

And so it came to be that, having served as a teacher and educational leader in various multi-cultural public school districts where the existing power structure did not resemble the families and students they were serving, the distant memories of when and how I had been the "other" came sharply into focus. I vowed to be a model of not only an educational leader but a moral leader. I remembered an earlier learning dating back to the third book of the Old Testament from the Bible—the Book of Leviticus. I was impressed with the challenge it posed to each of us, and was stunned to read that Holocaust survivor Elie Weisel once claimed to be able to condense the entire ethical teaching of the Bible into one sentence, "Thou shalt not stand idly by." How could one summarize so many years' worth of religious writings into a single sentence?

That became my motto – as a teacher, an educator, a researcher, and above all, a human being.

I will not stand idly by.

I will seek to use my power and my voice for what is just and right.

I will seek to understand what it means to be a child of God – one of the multitudes who are also his children.

I will see all God's children as my sisters, my brothers, members of my family.

I will not just stand there: I will by my actions consider my work as a holy commitment to lead a meaningful life of service to others – all others, including "the others".

When I discovered a lithograph created by famous American artist Ben Shahn, I purchased it to hang in all my offices all the days of my work to inspire me, to uplift me, to encourage me.

Now that I have retired, this work of art hangs in my home, reminding me of my life-long responsibility to seek to understand and to act, for as the Book of Leviticus taught me,

"Thou Shalt Not Stand Idly By"

As this extraordinary work of art continues to guide me, so do the remarkable poems of Jorge Prósperi elicit my respect and appreciation for his work as an educator, teacher, researcher, writer and exemplary human being. I fervently hope that Trenzas ~ Braids, his beautiful book of poems in two parts, will be read by a wide audience whose understanding and appreciation of those who come as "others" merge the richness of their historic culture with the inspiring story of those who came before and who welcome them now.

The Origins of *Trenzas*

Poems are born in the marrow of our bones. They slowly work their way into the poets' veins and flow through the heart where they palpitate and resonate. They wind their way into the lungs, inhaling the air of experiences and identity. From the first primal gulp of air, to every breath thereafter, poems are exhaled to provoke and evoke emotions. They articulate the inarticulable and ponder what the mind, heart and spirit need to stay alive. For the poet - poems are life itself.

Trenzas came to life during my infancy watching my grandmother brush and braid my mother's hair and my mother brush and braid her sisters' long black hair. Braiding was a time to ask and answer questions, for storytelling, sharing wisdom and always a time for caring and loving. There was an intimacy about it all that always finished with *besos (*kisses), *abrazos* (hugs), and with a resounding emphatic *¡Cuídate!* (Be careful!) - especially by the older braiders who knew the reasons why caution needed to be ever present.

Every woman wore her *trenzas* with pride and dignity. There was a sameness and yet singularness as *trenzas* danced in the wind behind them with a story to tell. I remember how beautiful they were . . . especially my mother's *trenzas* . . . how they made me feel safe and loved.

This book is divided into two parts. The first part of the book *En Sus Voces* (in their voices) represents the voices of Latinos/as who came into my life as part of my dissertation. The second part, *En Mi Voz* (in my voice) are original poems built on personal experiences of dual cultural identities born from the blend of my native Argentina and my diasporic experiences in the United States.

En Sus Voces Ensayo ~ (In Their Voices Essay)

It is said that the doctoral process should augment and contribute to the body of knowledge being studied. While this is a worthy goal, one never knows the personal impact that the process elicits for each doctoral candidate. For me, qualitative research became a journey where process, findings and lingering reverberations exceeded expectations. The required academic challenges dealing with courses, time and effort were expected and accepted. Right from the beginning, the focus was clear that it would be about immigrants, parents, their children, schooling and what parental involvement meant from the immigrant perspective. The process began with the tedious but necessary search for willing participants, protecting their identities, developing critical questions, doing audio interviews in Spanish, transcribing the interviews and translating each interview into English. It was an unrelieved and time consuming process with language being at the core.

All was moving as planned when during the latter stages of my dissertation, Mexican immigrant parents and their involvement in urban schooling: An application of Latina /o Critical Theory (2007), it became evident that there was a major missing link. The interviews were the core of the participant's conceptualization of parental involvement as it applied to schooling, life and their unequivocal love for their children. The life of the study was the authentic expression of the language . . . its meaning . . . its purpose. However, the interviews that were at the center of the study had gone silent. The dissertation was nearly finished, yet it called for the voices to take center stage, but the curtain remained closed.

There came a point in the dissertation when the countless pages of transcriptions and translations rested on my desk as a tome of qualitative research. There it was - page after page of language subjected to domain and taxonomic analysis - componential analysis - the systematic search for the attributes and meanings associated with cultural categories - coding and inventorying language to unearth meaning. It was all there; over 1,000 pages for anyone to read. But what was not there were the pauses when meaning was accented by eyes and voices of the participants explaining cultural idioms - slices of human gradations.

The dissertation followed an academic structured process. Latino/a Critical Theory and the Critical Research Paradigm were used to conceptualize the meaning of parental involvement of Mexican immigrant parents in the schooling of their children. Latino/a parents who were recent immigrants were unfamiliar with the educational process in the United States and raised their children with different expectations regarding parental involvement and schooling. Concurrently, traditional interpretations of parental involvement were based on conventional dominant educational ideology that projected what knowledge was valued or not valued - what was significant or insignificant. The study refuted the notion that conventional educational interpretations were neutral; to the contrary, I argued that they were born of deficit-learned paradigms and distorted epistemological constructs.

Consequently, schools' stock definitions and characterization of parental involvement were in conflict with the subtexts of what parental involvement meant from the Latino/a parent perspectives and beliefs. The dissertation addressed the question of what knowledge was recognized, valued and validated within the context of social inequality pertaining to equal educational opportunities of worth (Howe, K. R. 1993, 2007). El valor (the worth) of an opportunity was key as opportunities are not opportunities unless pro-actively made accessible to those who without choice and by design are situated in adverse socio-economic-political spaces.

The participants reacted to questions developed to coincide with the objectives of the study. But the planned questions and answers were only a starting point. It quickly became apparent that confirmability of the nuances of idiomatic phrases required adjournments to reread, rewind the tape, re-listen and reinterview to clarify meaning. An example was when one of the participants mentioned la mirada (the look.) The word and concept was repeated by other participants which meant going back to the tapes, transcripts and translations to find context. Also, what question(s) had been asked before and after the term was used?

Re-interviewing each participant that had used the word provided deeper meaning by way of synonyms and antonyms. Context clarified and endorsed meaning. Perspectives and examples were enhanced as to the why, when, where, how and impact on personal feelings. How were these participants left to deal with the meaning of la mirada (the look) upon seeing and feeling it? Was it real or imagined? Did it matter if more than one participant felt it? Wasn't it all dealing with intangibles and subjective perceptions? To what degree did it matter if they felt la mirada disrespecting and targeting the value and dignity of their children? The more I tried to disprove notions, the more la mirada was actualized and confirmed as to perceived intent.

To write the transcriptions, translate the words, find the domains, do the taxonomy and componential analyses led to findings, but there were still missing components that I felt were part of the data. What was missing was the spiritual golpe (the emphasis) of the expression - the vitality of the phrasing, the richness of passion that could only be felt as one human being divulges their intimate feelings to another. How does a researcher provide the intimacy of the moment? How does the researcher express a mother's tears as she described the racism and bigotry that her son faced by way of school staff and teachers? And most challenging, how does a researcher make available to readers those undercurrents of lingering multigenerational and intragenerational trauma (Danielli, 1998) and soul wounds (Duran & Duran, 1995)?

Each participant took on singular importance breaking away from the socio-cultural-political collective nouns of immigrants, illegals, aliens, unauthorized, day/night crossers and/or the undocumented. The participants provided awareness of the exhausting immigration journey, the consequent migrations throughout the United States; each one was a new starting point with constant challenges of finding housing, adjusting to new communities, dealing with transportation and securing jobs. While dealing daily with such inconsistent life-changing realities, the families had to deal with the demanding process of finding schools for their children, learning a different system of schooling and confronting new definitions of parental involvement. All of these responsibilities were ever present and had to be addressed with the challenges of dealing with the English language; the Anglophone idiom became a constant wall to comprehension and expression.

The most insidious reality was the constant awareness of fear mongering at their expense; racism, xenophobia and jingoism being echoed politically by a perplexed society going through its own painful cathartic process of dealing with the legacy of overt and covert social constructs. Each interview provided opportunities for parents to express redeeming counterstories, intimate feelings about their beliefs, values, their perspectives on education, how they defined Latino/a Parental Involvement and their unequivocal dedication, support and love for their children.

Throughout the dissertation, the analysis of the participant's language was impacted by expressions of lament, grief and sorrow. There was a constant inner voice that at times emerged to let me into spaces that could not be left unarticulated. The search to capture the embedded subtexts that were being expressed emerged by way of Poetics. This vehicle and tool made available a distillation of meanings by the participants. The process that I followed was guided by my lead advisor at Wayne State University, Dr. Karen Tonso, who through the Advanced Research Methods Courses made available references (Glesne, 1997; Mears, 2005; Richardson, 2002).

Therefore, I decided to create Poetics by using an original design that would provide the reader with the connotations and the nuances that the participants had repeatedly shared in their voices. The Poetics put human faces on those who lived the depredation. The poems were born from the counterstories as those presented by Gerardo López (1999) who used the perspective of Chicano migrant workers in order to provide alternate dimensions of parental involvement dealing with ethical stories of desperate vidas (lives). Vidas that go unnoticed, as if they do not count, but are unearthed by ethnographers, like Leo Chavez, whose portrayal of Shadowed Lives (1998) provides us with glimpses of subsistence and hardship, while combining analysis and depictions of survival. Marianne Exum Lopez contributes yet another illustration of clashes between home and school in stories warning that When Discourses Collide (1999) it is the children who suffer between the dominant mainstream discourses of power and those of marginalized children. This crucial point is brought into the classroom by Lisa Delpit's poignant book Other People's Children: Cultural Conflicts in the Classroom (1999) illustrating the divide between white teachers and other people's children of color.

Mears (2005, 2006) addressed the phenomenon of Poetics in her study of the Columbine High School tragedy where she documented a 'cloak' families developed in order to protect themselves from intruders - a blanket of safety to shield themselves from the lingering grief left suspended by conventional inquiry. Her design in qualitative research known as the gateway approach extracted words from transcripts as data condensing and distilling the message in order to present that message directly to the reader without relying on the researcher's summary or interpretation. Like Mears and other qualitative researchers, I sensed the constant emotional responses and therefore decided to combine Mears' method of extracting words from transcripts as data condensing and distilling the message, as well as the use of transcription and poetic display (Glesne, 1997; Mears, 2006; Miles & Huberman, 1994; Richardson, 1992, 2002) in order to access the nuances of meanings related to the Latino/a families, their children and *sus vidas* (their lives) . . . *en sus voces* (in their voices).

Poética ~ En sus voces

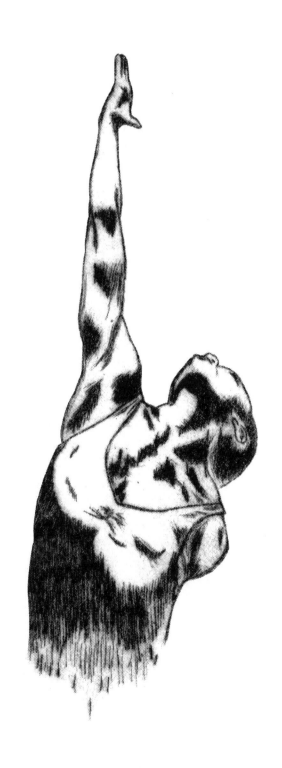

La Vida en Méjico

¡Dura!
Muchos viven sin esperanza . . .
Sin saber . . .
¿Por qué? . . . ¿Por qué?
¿Por qué? . . . Ya no pregunto más ¿por qué? . . .
Los güeros no entienden . . .
Vacacionando sin vernos . . .
Somos de orígenes humildes . . .
De pueblitos . . . ranchitos . . . chacras chiquitas . . .
Es difícil describir y entender . . .
Los americanos ni lo pueden soñar . . .
Vivir en un estado de desesperación . . .
Algunos sin luz, sin agua, sin nada . . .
Todo eso es un lujo . . .
Se aprende trabajar con sus manos . . .
No hay trabajo que sea muy pesado o duro . . .
Trabajamos de sol a sol . . .
La escuela es solo un sueño . . .
Duele soñarlo . . .
Yo nada más hasta el grado seis . . .
Yo era el más joven . . .
Ser el más joven es una ventaja . . .
Y fue mucho . . . los mayores . . . sin escuela . . .
Los mayores destinados al trabajo duro . . .
Ellos se sacrifican para los jóvenes . . .
Ellos saben lo que tienen que hacer . . .
Es como una tradición . . .
No nos olvidamos de ellos . . .
La vida en Méjico para nosotros no es una vacación . . .
Como creen muchos güeros que visitan . . .
Nosotros no tenemos vacaciones . . .
El sol nos golpea sin sombra . . .
Para nosotros . . . es una realidad dura y amarga . . .

Life in Mexico

Harsh!
Many live without hope . . .
Without knowing . . .
Why? . . . Why?
Why? . . . I no longer ask why? . . .
White people don't understand . . .
Vacationing without seeing us . . .
We are of humble origins . . .
From little towns . . . hamlets . . . small farms . . .
It's difficult to describe and understand . . .
The Americans can't even dream of it . . .
To live in a state of desperation . . .
Some without light, without water, without anything . . .
All of that is a luxury . . .
One learns to work with their hands . . .
There is no work that is too heavy or hard . . .
We work from sunrise to sunset . . .
Schooling is but a dream . . .
Painful to dream of it . . .
I only went to school until grade 6 . . .
I was the youngest . . .
To be the youngest is an advantage . . .
That (grade 6) was a lot . . . for the older ones . . . without schooling . . .
The older ones destined to hard labor . . .
They sacrifice for the younger ones . . .
They know what they have to do . . .
It's like a tradition . . .
We never forget them . . .
Life in Mexico for us is not a vacation . . .
As it is to many white people who visit . . .
We do not have vacations . . .
The sun beats upon us without shade . . .
For us . . . it's a harsh and bitter reality . . .

Desgraciadamente ~ Afortunadamente

. . . de haber nacido aquí ya no satisfecha
Hay que haber más que cantos tristes del pobrerío
No puedo más oír de los de abajo
Estoy cansado de vivir abajo
Méjico es muy diferente que aquí
Hay que pagar la entrada
Es poco lo que se gana
Es bastante duro mantener la escuela y darle de comer a los hijos
Por lo duro que sea . . . los valores . . . siempre se exigen . . . siempre
Es una cuestión de valores morales
Yo pienso que ésa fue mi educación moral . . .
que me sigue . . .
me empuja . . .
ser pobre no quiere decir que uno no tiene valor
ninguno le puede quitar su valor
desgraciadamente hay mucha pobreza
desgraciadamente no tenemos mucho
pero afortunadamente somos honrados
y eso es algo que ninguno le puede quitar

Unfortunately ~ Fortunately

. . . to have been born here no longer satisfies
There must be more than sad songs about the poor
I no longer want to hear about those at the bottom
I am tired of living at the bottom
Mexico is very different than here
One has to pay the entrance fee
One earns very little
It's very hard to sustain the schooling and feeding of the children
Regardless of how difficult it may be . . . the values . . . always emphasized . . . always
It's a question of moral values
I think that this was the moral education . . .
that follows me . . .
it pushes me . . .
to be poor does not mean to be without value
no one can take your value away from you
unfortunately there is much poverty
unfortunately we do not have many things
but fortunately we are honorable
and that is something no one can take from you

Pobreza

En Méjico hay mucha gente pobre . . .
los pobres son pobres . . .
no tienen bastante para comer . . .
es una lucha constante . . .
no pueden comprar ni un pan . . .
un pan . . .
no tienen para vestirse . . . calzar . . .
sobrevivir . . . nada más . . . sobrevivir . . .
de nada sirven los planes . . .
porque uno no sabe lo que llega con el tiempo . . .
para el pobre mañana no tiene sentido . . .
no se lo que pueda pasar con mi familia . . .
ir adelante depende mucho de uno . . .
coraje, esfuerzo, ánimo . . .
es muy difícil explicar desesperación . . .
como vivir sin esperanza . . . ahogándose . . .
mientras viendo las caras de sus niños . . .

Poverty

In Mexico there are many poor people . . .
the poor are poor . . .
they don't even have enough to eat . . .
it is a constant struggle . . .
they can't even buy bread . . .
a loaf . . .
they don't have enough for clothing . . . shoes . . .
survival . . . nothing else . . . survival . . .
plans aren't worth anything . . .
because one does not know what time will bring . . .
for the poor, tomorrow does not have meaning . . .
I don't know about the future of my family . . .
to move forward depends much on one . . .
courage, effort, will . . .
it is very difficult to explain desperation . . .
like living without hope . . . drowning . . .
while looking at the faces of your children . . .

De Chiquita . . .

. . . todo empieza con inocencia
Es el primer capítulo
Entrar a la primaria con gusto para saber y entender
Todo algo especial - único

> *Para adultos vista diferente - mantener*
> *Cada día sin igual*
> *No es de bueno o de malo*
> *No es de bien o de mal*

. . . días pasan como nubes
Todo nuevo para criaturas
Explorando lo desconocido
Corriendo sin saber adonde

> *Para padres días duros*
> *Poco nuevo todo pesado*
> *Mucho ya sentido*
> *Hoy es lo que cuenta*

. . . es mágico ser jovencita
Diminutivos abrazando a todo
Llamada corazón y alma
Sintiendo valor

> *Mentores sin descanso*
> *Abrigando, alimentando*
> *Dando cobijo*
> *Solo un enfoque*

. . . jugando con mariposas
Nada obligatorio
Nada cuesta algo
Vivir sin deudas

> *Vigilantes manejando vidas*
> *Todo obligatorio*
> *Todo cuesta más*
> *Nada gratis*

Cuidando . . . protegiendo . . . posponiendo . . .

As a Little Girl . . .

. . . all begins with innocence
It is the first chapter
To enter elementary (school) with a yen to know and understand
All something special - unique

> *For adults a different vista - to maintain*
> *Each day like no other*
> *Not a matter of good or bad*
> *Not a matter of right or wrong*

. . . days pass like clouds
All is new for children
Exploring unknowns
Running without knowing where

> *For parents hard days*
> *Little is new but weighted*
> *Much already felt*
> *Today is what matters*

. . . it's magic to be young
Diminutives embracing
Being called my heart, my soul
Feeling validation

> *Mentors without rest*
> *Clothing, feeding*
> *Giving shelter*
> *Only one focus*

. . . . playing with butterflies
Nothing obligatory
Something costing little
Living freely

> *Caretakers managing lives*
> *All obligatory*
> *All costing something*
> *Nothing free*

Caring . . . protecting . . . postponing . . .

Nuestros Padres . . .

. . . mi mamá yo creo llegó al primero
. . . mi papá al tercero
. . . mis padres no sabían escribir
. . . casi nadie sabía leer bien en mi familia

Pero pienso que la educación que yo tengo . . . de mis padres . . . la valoro mucho
. . . porque soy una persona responsable

Ellos no tuvieron mucha participación en la escuela
. . . trabajaban

Eso es lo que me recuerdo mas que todo
. . . trabajaban

Me enseñaron que el trabajo era cosa buena
. . . sabemos trabajar

Me enseñaron de tener orgullo en lo que hago
. . . trabajamos con orgullo

El tipo de trabajo no importa
. . . trato de hacerlo lo más bien posible

La educación que tengo me la dieron mis padres
. . . me enseñaron a trabajar, ser responsable

Mamá nos decía . . . tienen que prestar mucha atención
. . . echen las ganas a la escuela . . . para que no vivan como yo

Yo creo que para mi eso fue mi educación
. . . me enseñaron como amar y poder dar de comer a mis hijos

Nunca digo nada malo de mis padres
nos amaban lo mejor que podían

Our Parents . . .

. . . my mother I believe got to the first
. . . my father to the third grade
. . . my parents did not know how to write
. . . almost no one knew how to read well in my family

But I think that the education that I have . . . from my parents . . . I value a great deal
. . . because I am a responsible person

They did not participate much in school
. . . they were working

That is what I remember most of all
. . . they were working

They taught me that work was a good thing
. . . we know how to work

They taught me to take pride in what I do
. . . we work with pride

The type of work does not matter
. . . I try to do it the best I can

The education that I have was given by my parents
. . . they taught me how to work, be responsible

Mother would say to us . . . you must pay attention
. . . try hard at school so that you will not live like me

And I believe that this for me was my education
. . . they taught me how to love and feed my children

I never say anything bad about my parents
they loved us the best they could

Intuirlo

Es algo que es difícil de explicar . . . quizás imposible para el que no entiende

Es entrar por adentro de un ser humano

Es inculcar con fuerza

Es afirmar que la educación es poder respirar

Es lo que se enseña bajo el techo

Es apoyo

Es responder a responsabilidades

Es como nos enseñaron a nosotros hacer

Es platicar con ellos sobre estas cosas

Es el explicar que sin letras van a sentirse menos que otros

Es como se apoya la educación, aquí en casa . . . con sus palabras . . . con palabras de mi esposa

Es más que visitar a una escuela

Es intuir esperanza

Es intuir el ánimo . . . de echar ganas

Es que se trata de sus propias vidas

Es seguir haciendo todo esto . . . porque es su futuro

Es de inculcar el espíritu de voluntad

Instilling

It is something difficult to explain . . . perhaps impossible for one who does not understand

It is to go inside a human being

It is to inculcate with strength

It is to affirm that education is to be able to breathe

It is what is taught under a roof

It is support

It is to respond to responsibilities

It is like they taught us to do

It is to talk to them about such things

It is to explain that without letters they will feel less than others

It is how you support education here at home . . . in your words . . . in the words of your wife . . .

It is more than just visiting a school

It is to inculcate hope

It is to inculcate the will . . . to try with effort

It is a matter of their very lives

It is to continue doing all of this . . . because it is their future

It is to instill the spirit of willingness

Por Sorteo

Desgraciadamente sin igualdad
Parece siempre para otros

Kinder, Educación Básica, Primaria, Secundaria,
Preparatoria, Superior, Universitaria, Maestría, Doctorado

Empieza todo con esperanzas humildes
Deseos no faltaban . . . sueños sin recursos

A la escuela puse mucha atención
Tan bonito ese caminito

Era muy bonita la escuela
Las maestras todas en blanco

"¡Una buena alumna!" me llamaban
Era un placer asistir

Le dan la lista . . . no podíamos
Exigieron dinero . . . había cuotas

Con el tiempo amiguitos faltaban
Pocos terminaban

Se da entrada para otros
Hermanitas y hermanitos esperando

Muy triste ahora pasar sin entrar
Muy triste tener oportunidades sin igualdad

By Chance

Unfortunately without equality
Seemingly always for others

Kindergarten, Basic Education, Elementary, Secondary,
Preparatory, Superior, University, Masters, Doctorate

It all begins with humble hopes
Desires not lacking . . . dreams without recourses

I paid attention to my schooling
How pleasing was that little walk

The school was very pretty
The teachers all in white

They called me "A good student!"
It was my pleasure to attend

They give you a list . . . we could not fill it
Money was required . . . there were quotas

With time friends were missing
Few finished

One gives way for others
Little sisters and brothers waiting

So sad now to pass by without entering
So sad to have opportunities without equality

Oportunidades Sin Valor

. . . *y en esas juntas que ninguno entiende hablan mucho de oportunidades*

. . . *como si uno tuviera ya muchas*

. . . *y nos hacen sentir como si fuéramos bendecidos por ellos*

. . . *como si fuera nuestra culpa que nuestros hijos no toman parte en todo que ofrecen*

. . . *ofrecen culpa . . . no más . . . nos dejan vacíos*

. . . *nos dicen que no visitamos, no participamos, no valorizamos, no cooperamos*

. . . *pero nos dicen sin escuchar . . . personas sin orejas . . . y nosotros sin voz*

. . . *y nos predican que tenemos muchas oportunidades*

. . . *pero oportunidad es solamente una palabra vacía . . . cuando las esconden*

. . . *cuando no es igual para todos*

. . . *cuando se queda callada*

. . . *cuando ofrece menos que más*

. . . *cuando insulta de vez de honrar*

. . . *cuando ofrecen clases para cocinar . . . no las buenas clases*

. . . *cuando los miran como jardineros mas bien que ingenieros*

. . . *cuando miran a nuestras hijas como domésticas, nunca como doctoras y abogadas*

. . . *cuando tratan a nuestros hijos como un bulto de animales*

. . . *cuando piensan de ellos sin valor . . . solamente para servir*

. . . *que digan lo que digan y crean lo que crean en sus malditas juntas*

. . . *que continúen hablando al viento en sus juntas*

. . . *una oportunidad no es verdadera . . . si no tiene valor*

Opportunities Without Worth

. . . and in those gatherings that no one understands they speak much of opportunities

. . . as if one already had too many

. . . and they make us feel as if we were blessed by them

. . . as if we were guilty that our own children do not take advantage of all that they offer

. . . they offer blame . . . no more . . . they leave us empty

. . . they tell us that we do not visit, participate, value, and cooperate

. . . but they tell us without listening . . . people without ears . . . and we without voice

. . . and they preach that we have many opportunities

. . . but opportunity is just an empty word . . . when they hide them

. . . when it is not equal for all

. . . when it remains silent

. . . when it offers less rather than more

. . . when it insults rather than honors

. . . when they offer cooking classes . . . not the good classes

. . . when they look at us as gardeners rather than engineers

. . . when they look at our girls as domestics never as doctors and lawyers

. . . when they treat our children as a clump of animals

. . . when they think of them without worth . . . only to serve

. . . let them say what they say and believe what they believe in their damn meetings

. . . let them continue speaking to the wind at their meetings

. . . an opportunity is not authentic . . . if it has no worth

Cuando en puro inglés . . . trago tierra

Nos invitaron y aqui estamos

En el templo de enseñanza

¡Qué maravilla!

Nos hablan sin parar

     Trago tierra y me ahogo.

Escuchamos temblando

Nos piden que hablemos

La boca sin saliva

La lengua paralizada

     Trago tierra y me ahogo.

Uno se siente un miserable

Quisiera desaparecer

Es un temor no saber

Somos como estatuas

     Trago tierra y me ahogo.

Y nos piden si hay preguntas

¡Si supieran cuantas tenemos!

Nos hablan sin entender

Una pared de palabras

     Trago tierra y me ahogo.

Sin idioma somos invisibles

¿No saben que solo adivinamos?

Como un poste aquí plantado

Cuando en puro inglés

     Trago tierra y me ahogo.

When in pure English . . . I swallow dirt

They invited us and here we are

In the temple of learning

What a marvel

They speak at us without pause

> *I swallow dirt and choke*

We listen trembling

They ask us to speak

The mouth without saliva

The tongue paralyzed

> *I swallow dirt and choke*

One feels a failure

Wishing to disappear

Not knowing is fear

We are like statues

> *I swallow dirt and choke.*

And they ask if there are questions

If they knew just how many

They speak at us without understanding

A wall of words

> *I swallow dirt and choke.*

Without language we are invisible

Do they know that we only guess?

Like a planted post

When in pure English

> *I swallow dirt and choke.*

La Mirada

¡ Sí! . . . ¡Es cierto! . . . ¡Existe!

¡Es el asco de la mirada!

¡Sí! ¡Nos ven diferente!

¡Es la repugnancia de la mirada!

¡Sí! ¡Uno siente la mirada!

¡Es el peso de la mirada!

¡Sí!, ¡Es algo real!

¡Es el desprecio con arrogancia!

¡Como si quisieran escupir!

¡Es lo que no dice y se esconde!

¡Es la cobardía!

¡Es el miedo que lleva!

¡¿Adónde la aprendieron?!

¡¿Quiénes se la enseñaron?!

¡No es cristiana . . . sin religión!

¡Sí! ¡Sí! . . . es como miran a nuestros hijos!

¡Sin compasión . . . fria . . . sin ternura!

¡Como si quisiéramos robarle su blancura!

¡Ellos manejan y cuidan bien su igualdad!

¡Es la mirada de privilegio y derechos!

30

The Look

Yes! . . . It is true! . . . It exists!

It's the repulsiveness of the look!

Yes! They see us differently!

It's the repugnancy of the look!

Yes! One feels the look!

It is the weight of the look!

Yes! It is something real!

It is disdain with arrogance!

As if they want to spit!

It is what is not said and hides!

It is the cowardice!

It is the fear that it carries!

Where did they learn it?

Who taught it to them?

It is not Christian . . . without religion!

Yes! Yes! . . . it's the way they look at our children!

Void of compassion . . . cold . . . without tenderness!

As if we want to steal their whiteness!

They manage and protect well their sameness!

It is the look of privilege and entitlements!

Parental Involvement: En Nuestras Voces

¿Ha oido usted las palabras . . . la frase . . . parental involvement?

No creo que he oido de eso . . . ¿se trata algo de padres?

¿O quizás quiere decir . . . ¡no sé en inglés! . . . quizás quiere decir . . .

*¿De involucrarse
en las vidas de los hijos? . . .*

*¿De comunicar
sobre la vida de los hijos? . . .*

*¿De ser responsables
por la vida de los hijos? . . .*

*¿De apoyar económicamente
a las vidas de los hijos? . . .*

*¿De respetar
las vidas de los hijos? . . .*

*¿De tener salud en todo
en la vida de los hijos? . . .*

*¿De enseñar valores
a los hijos? . . .*

y que . . .

¡echen ganas! . . .

¡sean animados! . . .

¡sean guiados! . . .

¡respeten a otros! . . .

¡sean amados! . . .

¡Eso es lo que yo creo! . . . ¿Qué cree usted?

Parental Involvement: In Our Voices

Have you heard of the word or phrase parental involvement?

I don't think that I have heard of that . . . something about parents?

Or perhaps it means . . . I don't know in English! . . . perhaps it means . . .

*to be involved
in the lives of the children? . . .*

*to communicate
about the lives of the children? . . .*

*to be responsible
for the lives of the children? . . .*

*to support financially
the lives of the children? . . .*

*to respect
the lives of the children? . . .*

*to have health in all things
related to the lives of the children . . .*

*to teach values
to the children? . . .*

and that . . .

they learn to work with effort! . . .

be encouraged! . . .

be guided! . . .

respect others! . . .

be loved! . . .

That is what I believe! . . . What do you believe?

Respeto . . .

La palabra lleva mucho peso . . .

Pues es como lo van criando . . .

> *a cada uno de nosotros . . .*

El aspecto moral . . .

> *el valor más fuerte . . .*

Los papás me enseñaron a respetar . . .

> *pues se aprende por los padres de uno . . .*

Valores que se exigen siempre . . .

> *respetar a los humanos . . .*

> *nada más le dicen a uno . . .*

Sí . . . se respeta a otros . . .

. . . Sí, a la familia . . .

. . . Sí, a personas mayores . . .

. . . Sí, a sus maestros . . .

. . . Sí, a los compañeros . . .

. . . Sí, a todas las personas . . .

Porque uno tiene una cultura . . .

> *Un modo de haber sido criados . . .*

No cuesta respetar . . .

> *pero cuesta no respetar . . .*

Es conocimiento . . .

> *conciencia . . .*

Apreciar . . . reconocer

> *a las personas . . .*

Para aprender más . . .

> *avanzar adelante como una persona . . .*

Respeto es parte de ser humano . . .

Culturalmente . . . gracias a dios . . . ¡somos ricos!

Respect . . .

The word carries much weight . . .

Hence it is how one is raised . . .

> *each of us . . .*

The moral value . . .

> *the greatest of values . . .*

My parents taught me to respect . . .

> *hence by one's parents it's learned . . .*

Values that are always demanded . . .

> *to respect human beings . . .*

> *no more needs to be said . . .*

Yes, one respects others . . .

. . . Yes, to the family . . .

. . . Yes, to the elderly . . .

. . . Yes, to the teachers

. . . Yes, to your friends . . .

. . . Yes, to other people . . .

Because one has a culture . . .

> *because one has been raised this way . . .*

It does not cost to respect . . .

> *but it costs to not respect . . .*

It is awareness . . .

> *conscience . . .*

To appreciate . . . to recognize . . .

> *other people . . .*

In order to learn more . . .

> *to advance forward as a person . . .*

Respect is part of being human . . .

Culturally . . . thank god . . . we are rich!

La Frontera: Retumbos del Camino

. . . es un camino brutal, un viaje de una parte a la otra . . . para buscar una vida nueva
. . . la familia necesitaba irse de Méjico . . . no podíamos tolerar más

. . . irse es un sorteo . . . güeros creen que es una aventura . . . no saben
. . . necesitábamos irnos de México . . . nos daba pena . . . se llora mucho

. . . vine solo la primera vez sin conocer a nadie
. . . dejé a todos sin conocer a nadie . . . ¡a nadie! . . . ¡solo!

. . . uno no comprende, no conoce, se pierde
. . . decir que es una aventura . . . una luna de miel es una falacia . . . es una pesadilla

. . . a veces los niños pueden ser distraídos por lo que han visto
. . . ¡qué bueno fuera si serían cuentos! . . . pero es realidad . . . una desgraciada realidad

. . . riesgos, peligros, apuros, amenazas . . . olores . . . nunca olido . . . encima de mi cuerpo
. . . deja uno a sus padres . . . tuve que dejar mi esposa, a mis niños . . . esto es un pecado

. . . deja amistades, a su casita . . . humilde que sea . . . su casa
. . . deja lo único que uno posee

. . . se decide arriesgarse
. . . ¡de repente! dijo mi esposo

. . . ¿qué necesitábamos para irnos? ¿cuándo, cómo, cuánto, quiénes, dónde? . . . se sabe poco
. . . . se ven muchas cosas horribles . . . uno no tiene ni idea del horror

. . . mi hijo tenía sed pero no le podía pedir a nadie
. . . ¡ni en mis sueños! . . . ¡ni en mis pesadillas! . . . ¡se puede explicar lo que es cruzar!

. . . tanto caminar, esconderse, correr . . . sin descanso
. . . se oyen muchas cosas extrañas . . . mi hijo temblaba

. . . y todavía ahora . . . relámpagos, truenos, helicóptero, sirenas, tiros . . . todavía se esconde

. . . retumbos por toda su vida

The Border: Echoes of the Journey

. . . it is a brutal journey, a trip from one place to another . . . to find a new life
. . . the family needed to leave Mexico . . . we could not tolerate it any longer

. . . to leave is the lottery . . . the white people think it is an adventure . . . they don't know
. . . we needed to leave Mexico . . . it was painful . . . one cries much

. . . I came alone the first time without knowing anyone
. . . I left everyone without knowing anyone . . . no one . . . alone!

. . . one does not understand, does not know anyone, one gets lost
. . . to say that it is an adventure . . . a honeymoon is a fallacy . . . it's a nightmare

. . . at times the children would be distracted by what they had seen
. . . how good it would be if it were only stories . . . but it is a reality . . . an unfortunate reality

. . . risks, danger, fears, threats . . . smells . . . never smelled . . . on my body
. . . one leaves their parents . . . I had to leave my children, my wife . . . this is a sin

. . . one leaves friends, your home . . . humble as it is . . . your home
. . . leaves everything one owns

. . . one decides to risk
. . . with haste my husband said

. . . what did we need to leave? When, how, how much, who. where? . . . little is known
. . . terrible things are seen . . . not even an idea of the horror

. . . my son thirsts but I could not ask anyone
. . . not even in my dreams! . . . not even in my nightmares! . . . the crossing is inexplicable!

. . . so much walking, hiding, running . . . without rest
. . . many strange things are heard . . . my son would shake

. . . and still does . . . lightning, thunder, helicopter, sirens, shots . . . he still hides

. . . echoes for the rest of his life

Ganas

. . . y hay algunas veces discusiones solamente entre la madre y el padre . . .

De lo que se trata no se lo dicen a sus hijos . . . es entre adultos . . . privado . . .

Pero se sabe aunque de chiquita que lo que los padres
dicen es importante . . . ellos saben . . .

Nos amaban . . . había ganas . . . muchas ganas . . . daban ganas . . .

Con el tiempo uno sabe que platicaban de uno mismo . . . de hermanos y hermanas . . .

Son conversaciones que no se entienden hasta que uno empieza a criarlos como padres . . .

Y papa insistía y mamá reclamaba . . . siempre querían que atendiéramos . . .

Pero al fin, ninguno podía . . . y por eso es que los padres se desesperan . . .

Pero siempre hablaban de ganas . . . de querer algo más para nosotros . . . siempre . . .

Sentíamos sus deseos y esperanza . . . como ahora sentimos para nuestros . . .

Padres . . . hijos . . . quedándose con ganas . . .

Yearnings

. . . and there are at times discussions only between a mother and father . . .

Of what they are about they do not tell their children . . . it is between adults . . . private . . .

But one knows even as a youngster that what parents say matters . . . they know . . .

They loved us . . . there were yearnings. . . desires . . . the wanting was there . . .

With time one knows that they were talking about you . . . of brothers and sisters . . .

*They are conversations that are not understood until
one begins to raise them as parents . . .*

Father would insist and mother would solicit . . . always wanting us to attend . . .

But at the end, no one could . . . and this is why parents despair . . .

But they always spoke of yearnings . . . of wanting something more for us . . . always . . .

We felt their wishes and hopes . . . as we now feel for our own . . .

Parents . . . children . . . left with yearnings . . .

¡Todo!

¡Son todo! . . . ¡son todo en mi vida! . . . ¡todo!

¡Son todo! . . . desde el momento que nacen son los más importantes de nuestras vidas

¡Son todo! . . . mi hija es mi vida misma . . . ella es mi alma

¡Son todo! . . . para mi significan todo . . . por ellos sacrifico

¡Son todo! . . . para ellos se lucha cada día y a todas horas

¡Son todo! . . . mi hijo . . . su vida es por que se lucha

¡Son todo! . . . es por los hijos que cruzamos y sacrificamos

¡Son todo! . . . para ellos hacemos todo

¡Son todo! . . . para mi son todo . . . en una palabra . . . todo

¡Son mi vida! . . . ¿qué le puedo decir? . . . ¿cómo decirlo? . . . ¡todo!

¡Todo . . . todo!

Everything!

They are everything! . . . they are everything in my life! . . . everything!

They are everything! . . . from the moment that they are born they are most important in our lives

They are everything! . . . my daughter is my life . . . she is my soul

They are everything! . . . for me they mean everything . . . I sacrifice for them

They are everything! . . . it is for them that one fights daily and at all hours

They are everything! . . . my son . . . his life is why one struggles

They are everything! . . . it is because of the children that we crossed and sacrifice

They are everything! . . . it is for them that we do all

They are everything! . . . for me they are everything . . . in one word . . . everything

They are my life! . . . what can I say? . . . how to say it? . . . everything!

Everything . . . everything!

En Mi Voz Ensayo ~ (In My Voice Essay)

Listening to the experiences of the participants brought back recollections of my own personal journey as an immigrant. The personal similarities were based on the experiences of relocating as a young child with my parents, as we traveled from the rural lands of Argentina to New York City. For us, it was not a matter of crossing a border, but an ocean. In retrospect, I seriously question whether I would have had the courage to do what my parents did. It is only after reaching adulthood that I fully understood the essence of their audacity to seek a new beginning with a clear focus on my future.

Immigration is often thought to be unilateral, unidirectional, one step and one resettlement. The word "immigration" is nonchalantly used, with little considerations to its treacherous psycho-socio peripheries. The immense difficultly of the decision to immigrate does not take into account the daily anguish of rupturing ties with family, language, culture, region, friends, personal history and identity. It is a daunting leap of faith into unknowns leaving behind all that is familiar in the quest for a better life. Immigration begins with unsettling reasons why such a consideration is even contemplated. The weight of this arduous decision is life-changing, filled with apprehensions, unknown consequences and etched on the lives of those determined to make the journey. Therefore such decisions are considered over months and years; seldom seen as explorations or adventures.

My father was not politically motivated, as were some of his friends who had become freedom fighters becoming victims to Juan Peron's reign of terror. His perspective was that he had a family to protect but was aware of the ongoing oppression he had witnessed in the Patagonia working for large land owners. He called them panzudos patrones (fat cats) who traded their Patagonian bombachas (gauchescan pants) for their porteño (from Buenos Aires) English tailored suits but who ruled with the same absolute vicious power and control within city walls.

It was in a *pueblecito* (hamlet) that my mother and father met. She a criada (servant) - my father a man of many talents from farmer to sculptor - a simple-complex man with a deep sense of justice acquired from witnessing the oppression of *los de abajo* (those from the bottom). My father made the decision to migrate and then immigrate because he was not willing to exchange one oppressive life for another and had the courage and will to want for more. Family members and friends tried to dissuade my parents from leaving but that was not to be. Perhaps it was a matter of my family not having many possessions and therefore little to lose. We were not alone as many were fleeing Argentina to Paraguay, Uruguay, Chile and Brazil. Some for political reasons and others because they were part of the first wave of citizens who foresaw their rights dissolving. In turn, the government moved quickly to stop the exodus of intellects and workers while suppressing the press, unions and viciously eliminating freedom fighters.

During the planning stages, I was spared and protected from the backroom discussions. There was also the fear that I would share with friends information that we were immigrating. What were visible were my mother's tears without knowing why. Her entire family, friends and life, as she knew it, would be left behind. Other signs were the number of times family members would drop by to say goodbye. Why was there such sorrow?

The day of our departure was different as we quickly walked to the docks without speaking. It was all very different from what I had witnessed on occasions while sitting on my father's shoulders as arrivals and departures of vessels were always greeted by streamers and confetti with those on the dock and ship waving to each other. I was told we were going to go on a vacation and that we needed to move quickly. What I did not know at the time, was that this vacation was to be permanent and only one way.

The trip was not on a luxury liner, but rather a Swedish cargo ship. We lived for 10 days in a minuscule cabin next to the engines. It was all a clandestine enterprise arranged by my parents. My family arrived in New York during winter months. Moving from a temperate mild climate to the freezing weather of New York City was our first encounter with what would become a living metaphor regarding the new American culture - unforgiving and cold. The feeling of being a stranger was the new identity that came with no welcome wagon to greet immigrants. Upon touching American soil, migrations began with little time to rest, plan and feel safe. Asylum was desperately hoped for, hardly given and seldom expected. Strangeness and newness appeared at every corner.

After living in New York, it became necessary to move. The first migration was to the North End of Boston and eventually migrating to Detroit. My father eventually secured a job in an auto plant while my mother continued to find employment doing what she had been raised to be - a criada - servant. Moving and re-acclimating were part of an ongoing unsettling process always underscored by uncertainty. Each migration was a new encounter of living with fear, danger and surviving unknowns, with its own abrupt learning curve requiring courage.

The migrations were always connected to my father's pursuit for jobs. Each was unique accompanied by new unknowns. Such unpredictability was a constant weight while trying to capture a semblance of consistency. For example, how do we get to that place and back? Do we dare to leave the apartment? If we do, then what will we say if someone speaks to us? During this time my family lived in a state of economic uncertainty and I in an educational limbo. My father, who was not used to borrowing or soliciting help, was always trying to validate his talents by seeking to procure work. My mother was adjusting to the loss of her family and at the same time searching for ways to supplement the family income. My education was on hold as nothing was secured and dreams of opportunities began to turn into cold realities of isolation and one constant reality - survival.

Suffice it to say that my parents had a relentless work ethic that I observed and absorbed. Both of them took immense pride in whatever they did; from my father's woodworking, sculpting, construction, gardening and cooking - to my mother's house cleaning, crocheting, ironing and sewing for others. Work and the quality of their labor was a reflection of who they were. The other redeeming quality was that they never complained - never made excuses for their circumstances. They took ownership and responsibility for their choices and consequences. Resiliency and indefatigability were ever present throughout their lives - a gift they always made available to me.

I remember my mother's work most of all because she would take me with her on Saturdays and Sundays to discover her worth and dignity. She worked as a domestic during the week but left open the weekends in order to clean windows, garages, basements and huge attic closets made of cedar wood that housed prized animal fur coats of the affluent. I remember reflecting on the fact that some of the cedar closets were larger than my bedroom – so were the walk-in refrigerators where it was not uncommon to see a side of beef hanging along with a carcass of a suckling pig, lamb and frozen turkeys. I recall weekends when my mother and I would wait for three buses transferring our way from stop to stop to the suburbs called The Points - Grosse Pointe Park, Farms, Shores and Woods. The Points were 10.4 square miles - just 6 miles from downtown Detroit - might as well have been 600. The Points were known for their historical estates - homes to many of the national and international executives of the automobile industry.

Standing . . . waiting for those buses left an indelible image that I continue to remember – especially as I drive past solitary bundled figures standing at suburban bus stops during winter days. As I drive by I can't help but to wonder about their stories, their families and the children that may be waiting. For my mother, getting home did not mean that she stopped working. Upon arriving home she prepared our meals and then began washing and ironing for others and throughout it all sin quejarse (without complaining) – as if part of a natural process of being born and resigned to that status and class of being.

Irma Rosa Hernández Prósperi was a remarkable woman - exceptional human being. My mother's background, like many Argentineans, was a mix of native-european-mestizo origin. But it was her nativeness that provided her with substance and love for the land. Born in a pueblo with two birthdates (actual and official) she was raised to be a 'criada' which means to literally be raised to serve others. The serving would take place for those living in estates. The feudal pueblos were created in order to serve the hacienda owners and their families. Gauchos and their families worked to sustain the large ranches. My mother, who was the second eldest in a family of 13 children, was one of the many who was destined to a life of servitude. She once made a comment in jest that in Argentina she was known as a criada but that her title in America had been elevated to doméstica (domestic) but that when it was all said and done, the urinals all smelled the same. As one of the eldest in the family, this meant that she would face the reality of being trained and indoctrinated to serve as a child without the opportunity to attend school; the older children paving the way for their younger siblings.

Accompanying my mother to palatial Pointe estates seemed like entering a dream world where everything was magnified. Enormous rooms filled with furniture, often without anyone present. The deafening silence created an eerie feeling. It was like visiting a castle. So many different large paintings, statues, chairs, tables, sofas and couches. So many windows letting in the light - so many to clean. So many bathrooms to choose from - so many to clean. As we took the buses home, I remember being proud of my mother for being able to clean such large spaces. She was the one that left such estates smelling fresh, white shirts ironed and starched with precision, beds changed and food made to order for the week. It was amusing to hear, "Irma Rosa even irons my socks!" Didn't everyone?

Not only did she clean, sew, iron and cook, but there were always young children that would greet her yelling her name upon her entrance, running to her as if she had given them life. I was amazed how they crowded around her waiting for her abrazos y besos (hugs and kisses) . . . tugging at her dress until she knelt . . . touching her trenzas. She was the family's pied piper. The parents were amazed how their children understood her when she only spoke Spanish to them. Wherever she went, they followed like little ducklings. None of this surprised me. They quickly learned, as I had done . . . to recognize and trust her immense capacity to love. A love so deep that she made available to me within her womb. It was a satisfying feeling to share her as I knew that at the end of the day she was going home with me - she was mi mamá (my mother) and I was su hijo (her son) . . . and nobody could take that away from us. We arrived hand in hand . . . and we left the same way.

During those weekend trips, my role was to assist, stay out of people's way and remain quiet until asked to translate for my mother when the English became difficult. There never seemed to be enough time to do homework, go to the library, or experience the joy of learning for learning's sake. While education was often mentioned as a goal, the immediacy of survival tended to take precedence. I eventually fell into the official role of the family translator which became a necessary burden as it became apparent that my parents did not want to learn English. They avoided it like a plague. It was the same plague I faced at school. How does the simplicity and stability of Spanish vowels a, e, i, o, u make any sense when dealing with to/too/two not to mention threw/through, tow/toe, seen/scene - there/their. Yes, Spelling Bees were merciless. It was easier to just sit down, avoid the embarrassment and wish that perhaps one day I would figure out why there were so many silent letters that were never sounded out.

At home only Spanish was allowed to be spoken as my father often insisted, ¡Habla como te hicimos! (Speak as we have made you.) Therefore, as many immigrant children do, I became their lawyer, broker, agent and formal translator. The role of official family translator was an immense responsibility, particularly for pre-teens who were going through their own issues regarding their identity. It was all forced, yet accepted and expected as to what needed to be done. There was no time to be trained as there was no prior knowledge upon which to rely upon. Each encounter became an original learning curve with new vocabulary to be learned instantaneously.

Wherever my parents went, I followed. Thus, from a very young age, I was in charge of all documents, financial transactions, opening of every piece of mail, visiting the local bank to deposit funds (withdrawals were looked down upon), to the purchase of an automobile or a simple light bulb. I did not know it at the time, but watching them pursue opportunities and fighting through immense roadblocks provided me with elements of resilience. In a non-aggressive and pro-active manner, they were showing me what I would have to do in order to survive and perhaps not have to sacrifice as they had done.

One of the most difficult times as the family translator was when I visited the Henry Ford Hospital in Detroit to speak to a Hematologist who was treating my father for hemochromatosis and pancreatic cancer. I could tell that this meeting was difficult for the doctor as he asked me to inform my father that the treatments were no longer effective and that there were no more solutions. How does a child say this to a father? My father, as he often did, demonstrated a strength, dignity and integrity that remains with me. He sat up and asked how long he had to live. I translated and waited. The doctor felt that some experimental drugs could provide added months but could not promise. My father took a deep breath, smiled at me and said to inform the doctor that he was not going to die and that he had more time to live and for me not to worry. His focus . . . again . . . was on me . . . not his physical life . . . because I was his life. Again, he was right as he lived beyond the diagnoses. He also made sure that the prognosis would be carefully screened for my mother's ears and heart. On that day, I not only translated words, but translated what it meant to be a father and an honorable - noble human being. It was no surprise that the hospital staff and doctors always enjoyed his visits making them feel better and always leaving others with a smile. Others always seemed to be important to my parents rather than the me, myself and I. They were masters of selflessness. In this respect . . . as immigrants . . . they seemed to be humanizing the culture.

For us, life in Detroit was a matter of having to make constant adjustments rather than enjoying consistency and normalcy. It became a way of life that caused my father to long for what he had left behind as he sang the tango . . . Mi Buenos Aires querido, ¿cuándo te vuelvo a ver? (My dear Buenos Aires, when will I see you again?). As difficult as it was, the U. S. continued to provide tangible opportunities with advantages and consequences. My father would remind me that dólares cuestan dolores (dollars cost pain) and to focus on ganas (effort). The efforts were significant as we finally moved from an apartment to a house on the Eastside of Detroit. This was a major step forward. We now had more space - two bedrooms, a bathroom, small kitchen, a basement, garage and backyard. We were in heaven. The size did not matter - it was ours.

Educationally, my personal growth was placed on hold during my middle school years as I was classified to be a Special Education student due to my limited ability to speak English and to perform on standardized tests conducted in English. All tests to determine my intelligence and content knowledge were guessing games filled with anxiety and stress. To be in a Special Education Class was a traumatic nightmare, like being in a prison with invisible bars that didn't even dissolve during recess. All knowledge learned in Argentina could not be expressed and remained hidden. It seemed that silence was my best friend protecting me from further degradation and embarrassment - to say nothing was safer than to risk humiliation. It was much later in my life, while researching Bi-Lingual Education that I discovered that as an immigrant child I had been living in what is known as the "silent stage" of language learning - often misunderstood as shyness and/or lack of intelligence.

Much of the discovery process of life stops when language, the very medium of human interaction, becomes the enemy. Eventually, a middle school teacher by the name of Mrs. Beals recognized that my academic problems were not cognitive, but a matter of not understanding and not speaking English. I don't know if she was an administrator or not, but she had access to us and she seemed to know that we needed intervention. All the while my mother and father remained confused about their son's academic dilemma. How could their child be placed in a Special Education class that does not seem very special at all? How could their child in one country seem so bright and yet so lacking in another? Where had they gone wrong as parents? Their confusion was internalized and to a great extent they felt that they had failed me and that somehow all of this was their fault. Had the absence of their formal education been somehow passed on to me?

Parent–teacher conferences were avoided because of anticipating confused messages of failure and due to the fact that the meetings would be in English. My father quickly learned to stay away from the needless pain felt by a father who was denied taking pride in his son's schooling carrying the unfair weight of parental failure. Ironically, both parents unequivocally recognized, respected and valued education. They were the ones who had spent time pretend-reading to me as a toddler and had fostered a deep respect for educators – a teacher's word was sacred with the classroom a temple. When a parent conference was required, it was up to me to translate the teacher's messages of my failings and explain to my mother that I would not be able to move forward to another section or grade.

How does an adolescent describe such a message to his mother? What words does a child use to define and clarify his own illiteracy? During such Teacher-Parent meetings, there tended to be endless pauses between the teacher's English words and the Spanish translations that followed - the teacher waiting patiently until the translation was dragged through emotional and psychological barbed wire. I was always aware of my mother's body language when she would hear her own son tell her that he was a failure – all of this taking place in front of the venerated teacher. My mother's total body would cower with eyes that would swell. My mother's only option was to hide behind that standardized obsequious smile that shamefully holds back the avalanche of internalized tears when confronting dehumanization; the forced reticent smile that simultaneously reflects unjust shame, sadness and deep seeded anguish.

I was eventually placed in a transitional English class with other immigrants. We seemed to take up space and time seldom challenged cognitively. Once in a while, we were paraded in front of others in order to substantiate America's Melting Pot theory in action, the school's Little United Nations, or allowing others to profess their Color Blindness. In reality, our immigrant group was not part of the school as we were not allowed to participate in assemblies or special celebrations. The German woman who taught the class did not seem to be a teacher but rather a culturalist who provided us with projects that focused on melting identity and force-feeding acclimation – lessons going to the food store, a restaurant – always going somewhere to buy something. I can still remember the emphasis on "How much is that?"

All of the units provided a cluster of directed vocabulary that we would memorize and repeat as if memorization meant learning, thinking and inquiry. Mrs. Beals would extract me from the transitional language class and mentor me before school, during lunch and after school. She continuously made efforts to provide my mother with insight as to my growth. She was an educator-activist ahead of her time. She did not use me as a translator, but worked diligently to speak to my mother as a parent with respect and dignity. She did not speak other languages, but she provided an environment of safety and patience; with her the affective domain was not threatened and therefore the cognitive could grow. Mrs. Beals became my mother away from home. During the tough times she would always find a way to make the bitter sweet - a way to recognize and validate my presence. She took time learning how to say my name and felt comfortable doing so. She often commented that English, regardless of its many invisible phonetic mysteries and snares would need to be my number one focus. As she reminded me, "You will have to learn English better than those who teach it to you." . . . and then smile with a confidence that I could . . . and would. Mrs. Beals is the primary reason why I became an educator . . . to pass on that message of hope and promise . . . always with a confident smile . . . always letting my students know that they could . . . and would.

The tutoring continued throughout the school year and summer, to the point where I was able to attend high school, but my middle school years had been centered on catching up with English sounds and words at the expense of not taking Science, Mathematics and History classes. My High School years presented new challenges as there were always huge academic gaps that I eventually became aware of only during my adult years. Finally, I had to make a decision whether to go into the workforce with my father or pursue education. My parents intervened and made the decision for me as they expressed their sentiments of wanting me to continue going to school; a dream I had expressed as a young child. Their constant reinforcement was centered on "Serás el primero de nuestra familia." (You will be the first in our family.) I did not know at the time the depth and weight of such a perpetual reminder.

Regardless of the many negative experiences with schooling, they held on to the belief that education was the key to a better life. I entered Highland Park Community College, found new mentors and began my journey into a four-year college after twice failing the required English Proficiency Exam. A degree and teaching certificate led to a job teaching Spanish in Birmingham, MI. My hope was to be hired by the Detroit School District as I had done a successful one year student teaching experience at a local high school. Unfortunately, the district required citizenship status. I found it curious that the suburban schools did not have such a requirement or overlooked my non-citizen status. Surprisingly, suburban schools found my native Spanish speaking ability and foreign status an exotic and a 'cultured' attribute. I was valued as a classroom instructor capable of teaching the Advanced Placement classes as well as being asked to join the District's Multi-Cultural Alliance. This was a group of administrators, teachers and parents who felt that focusing on cultural differences had value. Before giving too much credit to the district for being progressive, the focus of the alliance was to promote foreign student exchanges and summer trips to Germany, France and Spain. Diversity literacy, social constructs and their social agencies were never on the agenda.

My family was thrilled - their son had graduated and was a teacher! Their dreams of their son attending school, graduating and being hired had been fulfilled beyond expectations. In turn, quality time was made at each personal graduation to make sure that my parents were present and that the diploma was handed to them. My mother receiving my Ph.D. diploma in 2007 . . . yes, with besos (kisses) and lingering abrazos (hugs) as she had done with me during those pretend-reading sessions on her knee. Yes, she would read to me without knowing how to read. She would read from the same book, but always different stories. As I always knew . . . "Qué inteligente es mamá!" (How intelligent is my mother!) . . . a diploma well earned!

Carrying a dual identity at a suburban school became a self-imposed daunting issue. Why was this happening? At school by day, I became George, shamefully avoiding any use of my Spanish first name, middle or mother's maiden name, while at night and weekends I was Jorge to family and Latino/a friends. The use of the name became an identity issue and flaw as I lived with double identities; one pretending to be European with ties to Spain and the other calling for validation of my own background. It was like living in two skins. I did not know at the time that the essence of my cultural authenticity provided by my ancestors and parents was being drained by the veil of passing for sameness, speaking without an accent and mingling with others for the sake of social status. It was all a con game being played between Jorge and George.

As a child I faced the challenges of the bilingual journey. As a young adult I was not prepared for other perplexing issues. It was during my late teens and early twenties that the emotional and psychological realities of being bi-cultural and living with multiple identities came calling. My perspectives and perceptions of the world and its people had been formed by my parents and family. They differed from American perspectives. How I felt and thought about the young, elderly, family, love and loving differed - not necessarily having to do with good-bad-right-wrong, but dissimilar. Not only were the two languages different, but at times in conflict as to cultural nuances. It was like entering and leaving two realities that were ever present. It also had to do with what I had been taught to value - the moral compass that had been shaped by grandparents, aunts and uncles. Definitions and awareness of power, control, entitlement, privilege, status, class, difference, otherness and justice were at odds. One generic answer, was "assimilate" - melt one core, become blind to the other and pretend. In other words, deny and suppress one cultural reality for another.

To live and navigate multiple identities can be a conscious and sub-conscious reality, as one is dealing with trying to understand self within the context of a multitude of socio-cultural elements and therefore the challenges are inward and uniquely personal. Every immigrant faces, to whatever degree, the challenges of dealing with multiple lenses. Which lenses determine emotion, behavior, belief and truth? The simplistic answer provided is often to ingest and copy. Assimilate to the language, to the culture, to "Who we are." "Become American - become like us." Wish that such answers were easily internalized without doing violence to the spirit of every immigrant who faces such a dilemma as a youngster and as an adult.

My personal multiple-languages/cultural identity journey was helped by not only reading about such a phenomenon, but by the wisdom of my dear mother who came to my rescue. My personal hypocritical teeter-totter game came to an abrupt end when my mother heard colleagues call me George, which I did not correct. She also noticed that I avoided using my middle and her maiden name as was the custom. She confronted me in her loving candid fashion by asking a simple question . . . ¿Qué nombre quieres en tu tumba? (What name do you want on your grave stone?) The question went to the heart of the issue ¿Quién eres? (Who are you?). Was I the convenient, simplistic George or the non-conventional and culturally complex Jorge Dante Hernández Prósperi? Who was I trying to please and fool? Her question made clear that I had tried so hard to buy in, that I had sold out. From that day forward, I knew my name. It is Jorge who writes the poems in the second part of *Trenzas*.

Poemas Íntimos En Mi Voz

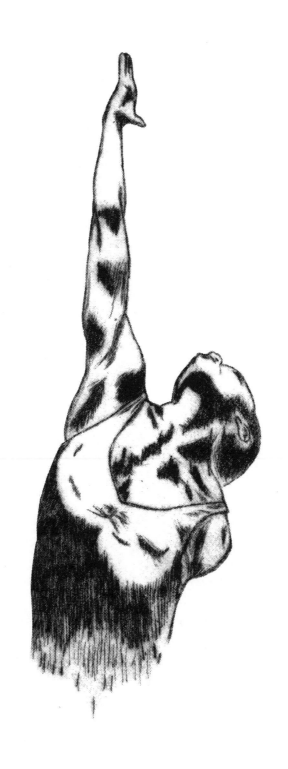

Trenzas ~ "¡Yo Soy!"

Trenzas nacen y crecen en chacras
Manos cansadas entrecruzando
Tres mechoncitos con cuidado
Frágiles entre dedos duros - amando.

Bailan a brisas infantiles
Con tiempo tocan al piso
Resaltando contra sol y luna
Brillando un negro azulenco - celebrando.

Cantan por atrás con inocencia . . . "¡Yo Soy!"

Una saluda a la otra
"¡Te veo querida!"
Bailando con harmonia
Juntas cuidando una a la otra.

Festejando juntas con identidad . . . "¡Yo Soy!

En silencio no es lo que parece
De repente cuelgan mudas
Raíces arrancadas del alma sin pedir
Lagrimas con ojos apretados - aguantando.

Se lavan ahora con desafió . . . "¡Yo Soy!

Resurrección de indignación
Se limpian . . . se cuelgan
Sin asco lucen de nuevo
Adhiriendo sin soltar - liberando.

Gritan de atrás con nobleza . . . "¡Yo Soy!"

"¡No te las puedo prestar . . .
No te las puedo dar . . .
Nunca ser tuyas . . .
Ni en tus sueños!"

Braids ~ "I Am!"

Braids born and raised in hamlets
Tired hands crossing them
Three locks with care
Fragile - gentle between stiff fingers - loving.

They dance to juvenile breezes
With time they touch the ground
Skipping against the sun and moon
Shining their black blue - celebrating.

They sing from behind with innocence . . . "I am!"

One greets the other
"I see you dear one!"
Dancing with harmony
Together one watching the other.

They sing from behind with identity . . . "I am!"

In silence all is not what appears to be
Suddenly they hang muted
Roots torn from the soul without asking
Tears with eyes shut tight - tolerating.

Washed now with defiance . . . "I am!"

Resurrection from indignation
They are cleaned . . . they are hung
Without disgust they shine again
Adhering without letting go - liberating.

They scream from behind with nobility . . . "I am!"

"I can't lend them to you . . .
I can't give them to you . . .
Never to be yours . . .
Not even in your dreams!"

Cuando Soltar

Mamá, papá sin saber, ni poder
Tareas - deberes que eran foráneos

El trabajo dominaba
Sudor de sol a sol

Pisos escolares nunca caminaron
Solo construirlos y limpiarlos

Cada día mano a manita
Ir donde espera el futuro

Al templo de enseñanza me llevaba
A la puerta abría su mano

"¡Aprenderás y sabrás!"
Un abrazo, tres besitos "¡Cuídate mi amor!"

Sin libros sabían lo que contaba
Para ellos "nunca" no se repetiría

Hacían lo que podían
Aguantando sacrificios otros sobresaldrían

Sin saber de letras nos enseñaban
Sin materiales creaban lenguaje

"Esa es una letra grande y esa chiquita."
Contando bolitas se aprendía

Ejercicios con las manos
Manos tiesas y tiernas

Esas manos hacían todo posible
Bien seguro apretaban

Y con el tiempo y cuidado
Sabían cuando soltar

When To Let Go

Mother, father without knowing, nor able
Homework, schoolwork were strangers

Work dominated
Sweat from sun to sun

Scholarly floors never walked upon
Only constructed and cleaned

Each day hand in hand
Going to where the future waits

To the temple of learning she took me
At the door she opened her hand

"You will learn and you will know!"
A hug, three kisses "Go with caution!"

Without knowing of words they knew what mattered
For them "never" would not be repeated

They did what they could
Enduring sacrifices so others would surpass

Without knowing letters they taught
Without materials they created language

"This is a large letter and this a little one."
Counting marbles one would learn

Exercises by hands
Hardened tender hands

Those hands made everything possible
So securely they hung on

And with time and caution
They knew when to let go

Tú Me Crees Sonso

Tú me crees sonso

que la noche es día y día noche

que ser empujado es lo mismo que resbalarse

que trabajar para otros es lo natural

que cada lagrima no cuenta si no es tuya

que la sombra elige a quien cubre

que el valor vale solo en tu imagen

que dios es sordo para algunos

que mentira es verdad y verdad mentira

que la esperanza no es mi opción

que oportunidades viven en tu bolsillo

que tener honra es tu derecho

que tus hijos y hijas valen más

Tú me crees sonso pero la sonsearía es tuya

Pero sin rencor te veo . . . sin odio

Triste lamentando tu ignorancia

¡Qué lástima vivir con insensatez!

¡Qué lástima vivir sin empatía!

¡Qué lástima vivir seco y vacío!

¡Que lástima vivir muerto sin morir!

You Think Me A Fool

You think me a fool

That night is day and day is night

that to be pushed is the same as to slip

that to work for others is the norm

that each tear has no weight if not yours

that shade chooses who it covers

that worth is valued if only in your image

that god is deaf to some

that lies are truths and truths lies

that hope is never my option

that opportunities live in your pocket

that to be honorable is your right

that your children have more worth

You think me a fool but the foolishness is yours

But I see you without rancor . . . without hate

Sadly lamenting your ignorance

How sad to live senseless!

How sad to live without empathy!

How sad to live shriveled and empty!

How sad to live lifeless without dying!

Epistemología de Obsequiosidad

Eruditos . . . ¡Basta! No vayan más a la hipocresía
Historiadores historiando de lejos . . .
¡Basta de su insolencia universal!
¡No más orgullo en revisionismo eurocéntrico!

¿Narradores? . . . ¡perjuros!

Nociones vagas de descubrimiento y salvación
Con orgullo creando ficción
De salvajes saqueando inocencia
Agua bendita bendiciendo asesinos

Curas siguiendo dioses de hiero sin curar

Descubriendo, salvando, liberando, civilizando
Dioses vestidos en acero . . . masacrando
Carbonizando humanidad nativa
Caballería andaluza rasgando pieles

Jesuitas sin saber a quien perdonar

Cruces tras espadas bendiciendo con cada tajada
Estaciones de la Cruz al revés . . . con carne y hueso colgando
Pisadas plumas quetzales choreando rojo
Deshumanizando bajo la sombra de la cruz

Amanuenses negando lo que sus ojos testificaban

Nonatos abortados entre vientres aplastados
Esclavitud bendecida por místicos fallutos
Exterminación echa forma de arte
Lenguas e identidades arrancadas

Etnógrafos falsificando horrores como si fueran la salvación

Epistemologia íbera validada
Ojos indígenas dogmatizados
Vistas obsequiosas hacia el suelo . . . no más hacia el cielo
Opresión, sumisión, esclavitud, servidumbre

Cronistas de lejos pintando conquistadores como héroes

Sin un susurro de la niñez violada
De amantes estropeados
De almas mutiladas
De la eliminación de la esencia de ser

¡Sin perdón y con vergüenza! ¡Arrodíllense antes su dios impío!
¡Cuenten a sus hijos y hijas la verdad! ¡De generaciones traumatizadas!
¡De fronteras artificiales creando falso orgullo!
No más engaños del encuentro noble . . . pero del cataclismo sin igual . . .

Epistemology of Obsequiousness

Erudites . . . Enough! Don't go any more toward hypocrisy
Historians historizing from afar . . .
Enough of your universal disrespect!
No more taking pride in Eurocentric revisionism.

Narrators? . . . perjurers!

Lazy notions of discovery and salvation
With pride creating fiction
Of savages sacking innocence
Holy water blessing assassins

Priests following gods of steel without curing

Discovering, saving, liberating, civilizing
Gods dressed in metal . . . slaughtering
Charring native humanity
Andalusian calvary ripping flesh

Jesuits without knowing who to forgive

Crosses following swords blessing with each slash
Stations of the cross upside down . . . with hanging flesh and bone
Crushed quetzal plumes dripping with red
Dehumanizing under the shadow of the cross

Holy men denying what their eyes witness

Aborted unborn among crushed wombs
Slavery blessed by false mystics
Extermination made an art form
Tongues and identities torn

Ethnographers falsifying horrors as salvation

Iberian epistemology validated
Indigenous eyes dogmatized
Obsequiously toward the ground . . . no longer heaven
Oppression, submission, slavery, servitude

Chroniclers from afar painting conquerers as heroes

Not even a whisper of violated children
Of destroyed lovers
Of mutilated souls
Of the elimination of the essence of being

Without forgiveness and with shame! Kneel before your godless god!
Tell your children the truth! Of traumatized generations!
Of artificial borders creating false pride!
No more falsehoods of the noble encounter . . . but of the cataclysm without equal . . .

Auto-Opresión

¡Qué fácil le hacemos el trabajo a racistas!
Le damos la victoria sin que nos demuestren su odio y vileza.

Sin ver su juego de mano para separar y conquistar.
Mientras corremos tras nuestra cola ellos nos pasan riendo.

Gozan cuando Cubanos pisan a Haitianos y Dominicanos
Celebran cuando Argentinos desprecian a Uruguayos y Paraguayos.

Se alegran cuando Chilenos ofenden Peruanos y Bolivianos
Disfrutan al oír el Puertorriqueño denigrar el Venezolano y Panameño.

Les gusta oír el Colombiano insultar al Ecuatoriano y Salvadoreño
O cuando los de Costa Rica achican a Hondureños y Guatemaltecos.

¡Qué fácil le hacemos el trabajo a los racistas!
Le damos la victoria sin que nos demuestren su odio y vileza.

Le ayudamos actualizar su ignorancia de quienes somos
Nos ponemos el mejor vestido patriótico para sentirnos mejor.

Perseguidos por nuestra misma opresión
Encarcelándonos, cerramos la llave de la celda desde adentro.

Sin látigos, sogas, y cadenas . . . negando
Autoemancipación, autodeterminación, autoempoderamiento.

Presumidos . . . culpamos a otros para sentirnos mejor
Mientras nos auto-oprimimos agitando nuestras banderillas.

Los racistas ni han levantado un dedito - ni necesitan
Sonriendo gozan de nuestra auto-opresión . . .

. . . mientras nuestros antepasados nativos lloran.

Self Oppression

How easy we make the work for racists!
We give them victory without showing us their hate and vileness.

Without seeing their sleight of hand to separate and conquer
While we chase our tail they pass by laughing.

They enjoy when Cubans step on Haitians and Dominicans
They celebrate when Argentineans denigrate Uruguayans and Paraguayans

They are happy when Chileans offend Peruvians and Bolivians
They delight hearing Puerto Ricans denigrate Venezuelans and Panamanians

They like to hear Colombians insult Ecuadorians and Salvadorans
Or when Costa Ricans belittle Hondurans and Guatemalans

How easy we make the work for racists!
Giving them victory without showing us their hate and vileness.

We help them actualize their ignorance about us
We dress in our jingoistic best to seem better.

Pursued by our own oppression
We imprison ourselves turning the key from the inside.

Without whips, ropes, and shackles . . . denying
Self-emancipation, self-determination, and self-empowerment.

Conceited . . . pointing fingers at others to feel better
All the while self-oppressing while waving our little flags.

The racists haven't lifted a finger - don't need to
While laughing they enjoy our self-oppression . . .

. . . while our native ancestors cry.

¡Qué inteligente es mi mamá!

Sentado a su rodilla ojos hacia su faz . . . mi lugar favorito.
Entre sus pechos . . . seguro . . . con su voz me abrazaba.

Viejas páginas arrugadas . . . tomos en sus manos.
Sagrados con el tiempo . . . hojas viejas . . . temas nuevos.

"¿Pronto mi amor?" . . . mi sonrisa daba entrada.

Cuentitos del gauchaje nativo . . . de chamigos . . . héroes todos.
De potros, Patagonia, y paisanaje . . . la familia dominaba.

Y leía . . . leía con tono y timbre . . . algunas veces paraba.
"¿Entiendes mi alma?" . . . mis ojos daban vuelta a la página.

Sin un día de enseñanza me enseñaba. Sin sabios designando letras.
Sin dominar lápiz ni pluma. Sin tareas ni pruebas.

Sin guardar rencor leía de mi destino. Que ayeres no esclavizan a mañanas.
Puro amor sin amargura. Lo que no fue suyo sería mío.

Antepasados siempre presente. Con estima los nombraba.
Entre lágrimas sus voces resucitaban. Y ya - otro abrazo fuerte sin saber por qué.

Y leía . . . "¡Esfuerzo y tu palabra son lo que cuenta! ¡Ser humano entre humanos!
¡Caminar alto y derecho contra el viento!" . . . "¿Comprendes alma mía?"

Y leía - a veces sin mirar las páginas. ¡Qué inteligente es mi mamá!
Sin leer leía. ¡Qué inteligente es mi mamá!

A puntos claves paraba. Ojos a ojos me contaba . . .
"¡Así es la vida mi querida vida!" Y otra vez me abrazaba.

A veces papá sonreía de lejos. ¿Qué sabía sin decir nada?
A veces se paraba con reverencia . . . mirándonos con ojos llenos.

"El fin querido mío!" . . . fines sin fin . . . de mañanas sin miedo.
De esperanza celebrada . . . de sabiduría internal y eternal.

Viejas páginas arrugadas. Sobreviven doctorados encuadrados.
Tomos en sus manos. Aguantando ayeres . . . ahora libre.

Hojas viejas . . . temas nuevos. Sagrados con el tiempo.
Resistiendo fines . . . todavía me lee.

"¿Pronto mi amor?"

"¡Sí mamá¡ . . . ¡Sí mundo! . . . ¡Sí vida!

How intelligent is my mother!

Seated on her knee eyes toward her face . . . my favorite place.
Between her bosom . . . secured . . . with her voice she embraced me.

Old wrinkled pages . . . tomes in her hands.
Sacred with time . . . old pages . . . new themes.

"Ready my love?". . . my smile gave entry.

Short stories of native gauchos . . . endearing friends . . . all heroes.
Of horses, Patagonia, and journeys . . . family dominated all.

And she would read . . . reading with tone and timbre . . . at times would pause.
"Do you understand my soul?" . . . my eyes would turn the page.

Without one day of schooling she taught. Without scholars designating letters.
Without dominating pencil nor quill. Without homework nor tests.

Without rancor she would read of destiny. That yesterdays do not enslave tomorrows.
Pure love without bitterness. What was never hers would be mine.

Ancestors always present. Pausing with esteem upon naming them.
Among tears their voices resurrected. And yet another tight hug without knowing why.

And she would read . . . "Effort and your word are what matters! To be human among humans!
To walk tall and straight against the wind!" . . . "Do you understand my soul?"

And she would read . . . at times without looking at the pages! How intelligent is my mother!
Without reading she read. How intelligent is my mother!

At poignant points she would stop. Now eyes to eyes she would read . . .
"Such is life my dearest life!" And yet again another hug.

At times father would smile from afar. What did he know without saying?
At times he would stand with reverence looking at us with eyes full.

"The end my dearest!" . . . endings without an end . . . of tomorrows without fear . . .
Of celebrated hope . . . of internal and eternal knowledge.

Old wrinkled pages outliving framed doctorates.
Tomes in her hands. Enduring yesterdays . . . now free.

Old pages . . . new themes. Sacred with time.
Resisting endings . . . she still reads to me.

"Ready my love?"

"Yes, mother!" . . . "Yes, world!" . . . "Yes, life!"

El Pecado Remordido

¡Qué pecado que los pecados se remuerden
Qué pecado que los pecados se aprenden!

¡Qué pecado pecar por años desesperados
Qué pecado caminar desamparados!

¡Qué pecado vivir separados
Qué pecado vivir enterrados!

¡Qué pecado que pardo, negro, blanco - solo quedamos
Qué pecado que fragmentando penamos!

¡Qué pecado que no honoramos a las madres
Qué pecado que ni notamos a los padres!

¡Qué pecado vivir encarcelado
Qué pecado no ser nunca validado!

¡Qué pecado sentirse marginado
Qué pecado nunca sentirse abrazado!

¡Qué pecado que no apreciamos a todos
Qué pecado que no caminamos a codos!

¡Qué pecado vivir tan triste
Qué pecado que la fe no existe!

¡Qué pecado que los pecados se remuerden
Qué pecado que los pecados se aprenden!

The Rechewed Sin

What a sin that sins are rechewed
What a sin that sins are learned!

What a sin to sin for years desperately
What a sin to journey helplessly!

What a sin to live separated
What a sin to live buried!

What a sin that brown, black, white - alone remain
What a sin fragmenting we sin!

What a sin that we do not honor our mothers
What a sin that we don't even notice fathers!

What a sin to live imprisoned
What a sin never validated!

What a sin to feel marginalized
What a sin never feeling hugged!

What a sin that we do not appreciate all
What a sin to walk at no ones elbow!

What a sin to live so sad
What a sin that faith does not exist!

What a sin that sins are rechewed
What a sin that sins are learned!

Corriendo Hacia Su Ser

Corrían hacia su ser
Gritando su nombre
Celebrando su llegada
De tirones a su vestido se arrodillaba.

Abrazos y besos - besos y abrazos
Más que suficiente para todos
Calmos ahora con ojos sonriendo
¡Había llegado!

Adultos la llaman la nanny
La nana, la yaya, la niñera
Llegan tarde para saludarla
Los chiquitos siempre ganan esa carrera.

Padres le entregan sus vidas
Ella sabe que preciosas son
Cuidarlos como si fueran suyos
Cuidarlos más que si fueran suyos.

Atendiendo la lista de hoy:
Lavar, limpiar, planchar, cocinar
Vestirlos, darles de comer, bañarlos
Levantarlos después de sueñecitos.

Vámonos de caminata"¡Hacia el sol!"
Platicando, explicando, enseñando
¡Todo en Español!
No hay por que no.

Chiquillos respondiendo, entendiendo
¡Todo en Español!
Jugando, corriendo, cantando
Cuentitos, rimas, siempre adorando.

¿Qué veían . . . qué sentían . . . qué reconocían?
¿Qué entendían?
¿Qué transcendían?
¿Por qué corrían hacia su ser?

Running to Her Being

They would run to her being
Yelling her name
Celebrating her arrival
Tugging at her dress she would kneel

Hugs and kisses - kisses and hugs
More than sufficient for all
Now calm with smiling eyes
She had arrived!

Adults call her the nanny
The nana, the yaya, the niñera
They arrive late to greet her
The children always win that race

Parents turn over their lives
She knows how precious they are
She watches as if her own
She watches beyond her own

Attending the day's list:
Wash, clean, iron, cook
Dress them, feed them, bathe them
Awaken them after little naps

Let's take a walk "Towards the sun!"
Talking, explaining, teaching
All in Spanish!
No reason why not

Little ones responding, understanding
All in Spanish!
Playing, running, singing
Stories, rhymes, always loving

What did they see . . . what did they feel . . . what did they recognize?
What did they understand?
What transcended?
Why did they run to her being?

Si Fueran Tuyos

¿Qué diferente sería si fueran tuyos?

¿Qué diferente sería?
Si fueran de tu sangre
nacidos de tu vientre
mamando de tus pechos
oyendo sus llantos
¿Qué diferente sería?

¡Qué diferente cuando no son los tuyos!
de tu carne y hueso
de tu piel marfil
de tu reflexión
de tu imagen
¿Qué diferente sería?

¡Qué diferente cuando valorizamos!
que uno es de oro y otro de bronce
que el pardo merece menos
que uno camina en la sombra del otro
sin conocerse uno al otro
¿Qué diferente sería?

¡Qué diferente cuando pensamos de igualdad!
que la infancia es la infancia
que todos son inocentes
que ninguno merece sufrir
que el mio es tuyo y el tuyo es mio
¿Qué diferente sería?

If They Were Yours

How different would it be if they were yours?

How different would it be?
If they were of your blood
born of your womb
suckling from your breasts
hearing their cries
How different would it be?

How different when they are not yours!
of your flesh and bone
of your ivory skin
of your reflection
of your image
How different would it be?

What a difference when we value!
that one is gold and the other silver
that brown deserves less
that one walks in the shadow of the other
without one knowing the other
How different would it be?

What a difference when we don't think of difference!
that infancy is infancy
that all are innocent
that none deserve to suffer
that mine is yours and yours is mine
How different would it be?

Nombres ~ Names

Vale el esfuerzo . . . ¡importa!

The effort is worthwhile . . . it matters!

"Jorge"

"What is your name? **Your name!**" "**What . . . is . . . your . . . name?**"

"Jorge"

"What?

"Jorge"

"Corky?"

"Jorge"

"Gorgy?"

"Jorge"

"Howie?"

"Jorge"

Horsy?

"Jorge"

"Giorgi?"

"Jorge"

"Too hard to say . . . whatever . . . We are going to call you José!"

"Jorge"

"What's your name?"

"Jorge"

"Teach me how to say it."

". . . . Jorge . . . jor . . . ge . . . "

"That's with a soft j and g . . . right?" "Jorge? Is that how you say it?"

"Sí, Jorge . . . "y tú?"

"I'm Saoirse"

"Sa . . o . . ir . . se"

"Close . . . Saoirse"

"Sao . . . irse"

"Closer . . . say . . . Ser . . . shah,"

"Ser shah,"

Yes, yes, that's my name!

"¡Saoirse . . . Saoirse!

"Yes Jorge . . . Saoirse!
It means freedom in Irish."

"Free . . dom?"

"Yes, Jorge . . . freedom!"

"Freedom!"

71

Nuestra Doctora

¡Llegó lo incredible! ¡Alegría sin igual! ¡Mira! ¡Camina con su sonrisa de confianza!

¡Mira! . . . ¡Mira . . . se lo ponen sobre su cabeza . . . mira, mira!

¡Mira! ¡Encapuchada . . . con ojos bien levantados!

¿Oíste su nombre? ¿Lo Oíste? ¡Y la nombraron Doctora!

Aquí viene . . . ¡mira que preciosa! ¡Nuestra hija! ¡Tu nieta mamá!

¡Pues no lloren . . . no lloren!

¡No llores tú! . . . ¡Yo puedo llorar!

¡Pues, lloremos juntos!

¡Mira . . . aquí viene!

¡Mamá, papá! . . . ¡Abuelita . . . no se levante . . . por favor!

> *¡Cómo no Doctora, yo me levanto para mi Doctora . . . Doctora!*

¡Abuelita . . . míralo . . . el diploma . . . lo realizamos abuelita!
¡No llores abuelita . . . hoy te graduaste también!
¡Es tuyo! ¡Y tuyo! !Y tuyo!

> *¡Ninguno te lo puede quitar Doctora!*

¡Gracias . . . sacrificaron mucho . . . tanto . . . gracias!

> *¡Con ganas siempre Doctora!*

¡Esta es nuestra hija! . . . ¡Mi hija! . . . ¡Doctora!

¡Por favor papá! . . . me da vergüenza . . .

> *¿De qué mi querida Doctora?. . .*

Es un título . . . enorme . . . pero solamente un título . . .

> *De ninguna forma Doctora . . .*

Es una palabra . . .

> *Si fuera solamente una palabra Doctora . . .*

Soy una entre muchas . . .

> *No querida, entre muchas eres única Doctora . . .*

¡Es incredible!

> *No, no naciste con el título Doctora . . .*
> *De chiquita lo creíste Doctora . . .*
> *No te lo regalaron Doctora . . .*
> *No lo robaste Doctora . . .*
> *Lo sudaste Doctora . . .*

Agradesco el homenaje . . .

> *Solamente hablo la verdad . . . y ahora . . . con respeto Doctora . . .*

Eres un amor . . . eres . . . ¡mi papá!

> **¡Y tú . . . mi hija! . . . ¡Doctora! . . . ¡Nuestra Doctora!**

Our Doctor

The incredible has arrived! Joy without equal! Look! Walking with her confident smile!

Look! Look they are placing it over her head . . . look, look!

Look they are hooding her . . . with eyes looking up!

Did you hear her name? Did you hear it? They called her Doctor!

Here she comes . . . look how precious! Our daughter! Your granddaughter!

Now, don't cry . . . don't cry!

Don't you cry! I can cry!

Ok then . . . let's cry together!

Look . . . she is coming!

Mom, dad . . . grandmother . . . don't get up . . . please!

Of course I will get up, I get up for my Doctor . . . Doctor!

Grandmother . . . look at it . . . the diploma . . . we did it together grandmother!
Don't cry grandmother . . . you also graduated today!
It is yours! And yours! And yours!

No one can take it away Doctor!

Thank you . . . you sacrificed so much . . . so much . . . thank you!

With willingness Doctor!

This is our daughter! My daughter! The Doctor!

Please dad . . . you are embarrassing me . . .

How my dear Doctor?

It is a title . . . enormous . . . but only a title . . .

Not at all Doctor . . .

It is a word . . .

If only just a word Doctor . . .

I am one among many . . .

No dear, among many you are one Doctor . . .

It is incredible!

No, you were not born with the title Doctor . . .
As a child you dreamed it Doctor . . .
It was not gifted to you Doctor . . .
You did not steal it Doctor . . .
You sweated it Doctor . . .

I thank you for the compliment . . .

Only speaking the truth . . . and now . . . with respect Doctor . . .

You are a love . . . you are . . . my father!

And you . . . my daughter . . . Doctor! . . . Our Doctor!

Opresión: Sin Premio de la Academia

Casticismo, Chauvinismo, Clasicismo, Discriminación, Esclavitud, Eugenesia,
Genocidio, Homofobia, Jingoísmo, Machismo, Prejuicio,
Racismo, Servidumbre, Sexismo, Xenofobia
Predisposiciones malignas
Nacen en pozos envenenados
Choreando de pus
Contaminado el aire
Con cada respiro deshumanizando.

Creencias, lenguaje, actitudes construidos
Aprendidas de infancia
Algunas tuyas . . . algunas mías
De los que valen y no valen
De inferioridades y deficiencias

Científicos, biólogos, antropólogos
Ilustrando quien es y no es humano
Americanus, Europaeus, Asiaticus, Afer
Separando, clasificando, categorizando
Taxonomía por color, humor, y postura

Para los validados . . . ¡Supremacía!
Para los de sangre pura mochilas gratis
Llenas de pasaportes, visas, cupones
Derechos, privilegios, preferencias
Solo para quienes reflejan la imagen

Es absurdo creer en el premio de opresión
Que sufrimos más que otros
Que el único dolor legítimo es nuestro
Que la opresión es exclusiva
Que la persecución es selectiva

Qué es un pecado mortal olvidarse
Que al despreciar a uno
Despreciamos a todos.

Oppression: Without an Academy Award

Casteism, Chauvinism, Classism, Discrimination, Slavery, Eugenics,
Genocide, Homophobia, Jingoism, Machoism, Prejudice,
Racism, Servitude, Sexism, Xenophobia

Malignant predispositions
Born in poisoned pits
Dripping pus
Contaminating the air
Each breath dehumanizing.

Constructed beliefs, language, attitudes
Learned at infancy
Some yours . . . some mine
Of those who are valued and not
Of inferiorities and deficiencies.

Scientists, biologists, anthropologists
Illustrating who is human and who is not
Americanus, Europaeus, Asiaticus, Afer
Separating, classifying, characterizing
Taxonomy by color, attitude, and posture.

For those validated . . . Supremacy!
For blood purists a free backpack
Filled with passports, visas, and coupons
Entitlements, privileges, preferences
But only for those who reflect the image.

It is absurd to believe in the Academy of oppression
That we suffer more than others
That the only legitimate pain is ours
That oppression is exclusive.

That persecution is selective
A mortal sin to forget
That upon disparaging one
We disparage all.

Coplas de un Payador Perseguido	*Couplets from a Pursued Minstrel*
Milonga Pampeana	*Pampean Song*
Por: Héctor Roberto Chavero Aramburú	*By: Héctor Roberto Chavero Aramburú*

Amigos voy a dejarlos	*Friends I now leave you*
Está mi parte cumplida	*My part is complete*
Es la forma preferida	*In the preferred style*
De una milonga pampeana	*Of a gauchescan song*
Canté de manera llana	*I sang in a plain manner*
Ciertas cosas de la vida	*Certain things of life*
Tal vez alguno se acuerde	*Perhaps someone will remember*
Que aquí cantó un argentino	*That here sang an Argentinean*

The couplets depicted on this page are verses from the extensive poem:
Coplas de un Payador Perseguido 1972 by Héctor Roberto Chavero Aramburú
also known as Atahualpa Yupanqui and Don Ata
His writings, often accompanied by guitar, were popularized
by payadores Jorge Cafrune, Mercedes Sosa, and Facundo Cabral
and now available by way of You Tube

The Significance of References

Upon entering the doctoral program and process, the members of the doctoral committee provided an astute focus regarding how best to deal with the *Literature Review* and general references. They said to always begin first with a thorough review of the bibliography that would provide meaning, purpose and intent. The references could lead to further discoveries of peripheries not considered and I was urged to pursue those critical connections.

The references being provided reflect the *Literature Review* of the dissertation *Mexican immigrant parents and their involvement in urban schooling: An application of Latina /o Critical Theory (2007)* associated with the poetics and are being made available to provide sources for those pursuing qualitative research through LatinX, Latino/a Critical Theory and the Critical Research Paradigm.

REFERENCES

Bonnilla-Silva, E. (2001). White supremacy and racism in the post-civil rights era. Boulder: Lynne Rienner Publishers, Inc.

Brown v. Board of Education, 347 U.S. 483 (1954).

Camarota, S.A. (2001, Spring). Immigrants in the United States – 2000. Specturm, 74, 2, 1-5.

Carrasquillo, A. L., & London, C. B. G. (1993). Parent and schools: A source book. New York: Garland.

Carrol, J. A tale that fiction would envy: Naturalistic inquiry methods in the visual arts. Abstract retrived 1/9/06 from http://www.aare.edu.au/02pap/car02530.htm.

Chang, R. S. (2002). Critiquing "race" and its uses: Critical race theory's uncompleted argument. In F. Valdes, J. Culp, & A. Harris. Crossroads, directions, and new critical race theory. (pp. 87-96). Philadelphia: Temple University Press.

Chavez, L. R. (1998). Shadowed lives: Undocumented immigrants in American society. United States of America: Wadsworth Thomson Learning

Chavkin, N. F. (1993). Families and schools in a pluralistic society. New York: State University of New York Press.

Chavkin, N.F. & Gonzalez, D.L. (1995). Forging partnerships between Mexican American parents and the schools. West Virginia: ERIC Clearinghouse on Rural Education and Small Schools. 4 pages. ED388489.

Chavkin, N.F., & Williams, D. L. (1993). Minority parents and the elementary school: Attitudes and practices. In N.F. Chavkin (Ed.), Families and schools in a pluralistic society (pp. 73-83). Albany, NY: State University of New York Press.

Cline, Z. and Necochea, J. (2001). ¡Basta Ya! Latino parents fighting entrenched racism. Bilingual Research Journal, 25: 1 & 2 Winter & Spring (1-25).

Commins, N. L. & Miramontes O. B. (1989). Perceived and actual linguistic competence: A descriptive study of four low-achieving Hispanic bilingual students. American Educational Research Journal. 26: 443-472.

Covarrubias & Revilla, (2003). Agencies of transformational resistance. Sixth Annual LatCrit Conference. Publication of Florida Law Review.

Creswell, J. W. (1998). Qualitative inquiry and research design choosing among five traditions. Thousand Oaks, CA: Sage Publications, Inc.

Crenshaw, K. W. (1995). Mapping the margins: Intersectionality, identity politics, and violence against women of color. In Crenshaw, K., Gotanda, N., Peller, G. & Thomas, K. (1995). (Eds.). Critical Race Theory the writings that formed the movement (357-383). New York: The New Press.

Crenshaw, K., Gotanda, N., Peller, G. & Thomas, K. (1995). Critical Race Theory the writings that formed the movement. New York: The New Press.

Cummins, J. (1978). Educational implications of mother tongue maintenance in minority language groups. The Canadian Modern Language Review 34: 395-416.

Cummins, J. (1980). The cross-lingual dimensions of language proficiency: Implications for bilingual education and the optimal age issue, TESOL Quarterly 14, 2 (June): 175-187.

Cummins, J. (1981). The role of primary language development in promoting educational success for language minority students. In Schooling and language minority students: A theoretical framework, Los Angeles: California State Department of Education, Evaluation Dissemination and Assessment Center.

Cushner, K., McClelland, A., & Safford, P. (2003). Human diversity in education. New York: McGraw-Hill.

Danieli, Y. (1998). International handbook of multigenerational legacies of trauma. New York: Plenum press.

Danieli, Y., Rodley, N. S., Weisaeth, L. (1996). International responses to traumatic stress. New York: Baywood Publishing Company, Inc.

Darder, Torres, & Gutierrez, (Eds.). (1997). Latinos and education: A critical reader. New York: Routledge.

Dauber, S.L., & Epstein, J (1993). Parents' attitudes and practices of involvement in inner-city elementary and middle schools. In N. F. Chavkin, Families and schools in a pluralistic society (pp. 53-71). Albany, NY: State University of New York Press.

Davidson, A. L. (1997). Marbella Sanchez: On marginalization and silencing. In M. Seller and L. Weis (Eds.), Beyond black and white new faces and voices in U.S. schools (15-44). New York: State University of New York Press.

Delgado, R. (1984). The imperial scholar: Reflections on a review of civil rights literature. University of Pennsylvania Law Review, 132, 561-578.

Delgado, R. (1995). Legal storytelling: Storytelling for oppositionists and others: A plea for narrative. In R. Delgado (Ed.), Critical race theory: The cutting edge (pp. 64-74). Philadelphia: Temple University Press.

Delgado, R. (2002). Critical race theory (Second Edition). Philadelphia: Temple University Press.

Delgado, R. & Stefancic, J. (2000) (Eds). Critical race theory the cutting edge. Philadelphia: Temple University Press.

Delgado, R. & Stefancic, J. (2001). Critical race theory an introduction. New York: New York University Press.

Delgado Bernal, D. (1998). Using a Chicana feminist epistemology in educational research. Harvard Educational Review, 68(4), 555-582.

Delgado Bernal, D. (2002). Critical race theory, LatCrit theory and critical raced-gendered epistemologies: Recognizing students of color as holders and creators of knowledge, Qualitative Inquiry, 8(1), 105-126.

Delgado-Gaitán, C. (1990). Literacy for empowerment: The role of parents in children's education. New York: Falmer Press.

Delgado-Gaitan, C. (1994). Consejos: The power of cultural narratives. Anthropology and Education Quarterly, 23, 298-316.

Delgado-Gaitan, C. (2004). Involving Latino families in schools. Thousand Oaks, CA: Corwin Press.

Delgado-Gaitan, C., & Trueba, H. (1991). Crossing cultural borders: Education for immigrant families in America. London: Falmer.

Delpit, L. (1992). Education in a multicultural society: Our future's greatest challenge. Journal of Negro Education, 61(3), 237-261.

Delpit, L. (1995). Other people's children: Cultural conflicts in the classroom. New York: The New Press

Dennet, D. (1984). Elbow room: The varieties of free will worth wanting Cambridge MA: MIT Press.

Denzin, H. K., & Lincoln, Y. L. (Eds.). (1994). The handbook of qualitative research. Thousand Oaks, CA: Sage.

Denzin, N. K., & Lincoln, Y. S. (Eds.). (2005). *The Sage handbook of qualitative research* (3rd ed.). Thousand Oaks, CA: Sage.

Deyhle, D. (2004). Navajo youth and Anglo racism: Cultural integrity and resistance. In Sonya Anderson, P. Attwood & L. Howard. (Eds.). Facing racism in education (13-56). Cambridge: Harvard Educational Review.

Diamond, J. B., Wang, L., Gomez, K. W. (2004). African-American and Chinese-American Parent Involvement: The importance of race, class, and culture. Harvard family research project. Retrieved on 8/5/2005 from http://www.gse.harvard.edu/hfrp/projects/ fine/ resources/digest/race.html

Dillingham Report, (1907-1911). The Immigration Commission Reports from the Dillingham Commission Comprising U.S. Serial Set numbers 5663 through 56843 and 5865 through 5881.

Du Bois, W. E. B. (1903). The souls of Black folk. Chicago: A.C. McClurg.

Dudziak, M. L. (1988). Desegregation as a cold war imperative, 41 Stan. L. Rev. 61.

Dunn, L. M. (1987). Bilingual Hispanic children on the U.S. mainland: A review of research on their cognitive, linguistic and scholastic development (AGS monograph). Circle Pines, MN: American Guidance Service.

Duran, E. & Duran, B. (1995). Native American postcolonial psychology. Albany: State University of New York.

Durodoye, B. A. (2003). The science of race in education. Multicultural Perspectives Journal of the National Association for Multicultural Education, 5(2), 10-16.

Eccles, J., & Harold, R.D. (1996). Family involvement in children's and adolescents' schooling. In J. Dunn & A. Booth (Eds.), Family-School Links (pp. 3-34). Mahwah, NJ: Lawrence Erlbaum.

Eiesner, E. W. (1991). The enlightened eye: Qualitative inquiry and the enhancement of educational practice. New York: Macmillan Publishing Company.

Eisenhart, M. (2001). Educational ethnography past, present and future: Ideas to think with. Educational Researcher, 30(8), 16-27.

Emery, K. & Ohanian, (2004). Why is corporate America bashing our public schools? Portsmouth, NH: Heinemann.

Epstein, J. L. (1986). Parents' reaction to teacher practices of parent involvement. The elementary School Journal, 86, 277-294.

Epstein, J. L. (1990). School and family connections: Theory, research, and implications for integrating sociologies of education and family. In D. Unger & M. Sussman (Eds.), Families in community settings: Interdisciplinary perspectives (pp. 99-126). Binghamton, NY: Hayworth.

Epstein, J. L. (1995). School/family/community partnerships: Caring for the children we share. Phi Delta Kappan, 76, 701-712.

Epstein, J. L. (1996). Perspectives and previews on research and policy for school, family and community partnerships. In A. Booth & J. F. Dunn (Eds.), Family-School links. Mahwah, NJ: Lawrence Erlbaum Associates, Publishers.

Equal Education Opportunities Act (EEOA) Section 1703(f).

Ferg-Cadina, J. A. (2004). Black, white, and brown: Latino school desegregation efforts in the pre- and post- Brown v. Education era. Mexican American Legal Defense and Educational Fund. http://www.maldef.org/publications/pdf/LatinoDesegregationPaper 2004.pdf

Fields, B. (2003). The historical origins and development of racism. In Race – The Power of an illusion. [Newsreel]. California, U.S. Retrieved 11/30/2004 from www.pbs.org/race/000_About/002_04--background-02-01.htm

Fine, M. (1991). Framing dropouts. New York: State University of New York Press.

Fine, M., Weis, L., & Addelston, J. & Marusza, J. (1997). White loss. In M. Seller & L. Weis, Beyond black and white: New faces and voices in U.S. schools (283-301). New York: State University of New York Press.

Fordham, S. (1996). Blacked out: Dilemmas of race, identity, and success at Capital High. Chicago: The University of Chicago Press.

Fordham, S. (1997). "Those loud black girls": (Black) women, silence, and gender "passing" in the academy. In M. Seller & L. Weis, Beyond Black and white new faces and voices in U.S. schools (81-111). New York: State University of New York Press.

Fordham, S. & Ogbu J. U. (1986). Black students' school success: Coping with the "burden of 'acting white'" Urban Review, 18(3):176-206.

Frankenberg, E. Lee, D., & Orfield, G. (2003), January). A multiracial society with segregated schools: Are we losing the dream? Cambridge, MA: The Civil rights Project, Harvard University.

Franciosi, R. J. (2004). The rise and fall of American Public Schools. Westport, CT: Praeger Publishers.

Fredrickson, G. (2003). The historical origins and development of racism. In race – The power of an illusion. [Newsreel]. California, U.S. Retrieved 11/30/2004 from www.pbs.org/race/000_About/002_04--background-02-01.htm

Freire, P. (1972). Pedagogy of the oppressed. New York: The Continuum International Publishing Group, Inc.

Freire, P. (1973). Education as the practice and freedom in education for critical consciousness. New York: Continuum.

Friend, R. A. (1993). Choices, not closets: Heterosexism and homophobia in schools. In L. Weis & M. Fine (Eds.) Beyond silenced voices (pp. 209-236). Albany: State University of New York Press.

Furstenberg, F. F. Jr., Cook, T. D., Eccles, J., Elder, Jr., Sameroff, A. (1999). Managing to make it. Chicago: University of Chicago Press.

Gay, G. (1988). Designing relevant curricula for diverse learners. Education and Urban Society, 20, 327-340.

Gay, G. (1991). Culturally diverse students and social studies. In J.P. Shaver (Ed.), Handbook of research on social studies teaching and learning (pp. 144-156). New York: Macmillan.

Gay, G. (1992). The state of multicultural education in the United States. In K. A. Moodley (Ed.), Beyond the multicultural education: International perspectives (pp. 41-65). Calgary, Alberta: Detsetting Enterprises.

Gay, G. (1994). A synthesis of scholarship in multicultural education. NCREL's Urban Education Program. http://www.ncrel.org/sdrs/areas/issues/educatrs/leadrshp/le0gay.htm

Gay, G. (1995). Mirror images on common issues: Parallels between multicultural education and critical pedagogy. In D. E. Sleeter & P. MacLaren (Eds.), Multicultural education, critical pedagogy, and the politics of difference (pp. 155-190). Albany: State University of New York Press.

Gay, G. (2004). Curriculum theory and multicultural education. In Banks, A. J. & McGee Banks, (Eds.). Handbook of research on multicultural education. San Francisco: John Wiley & Sons.

Geertz, C. (1973, 2000). The interpretation of cultures. New York: Basic Books.

Geertz, C. (1995). After the fact: Two countries, four decades, one anthropologist. Cambridge, MA: Harvard University Press.

Gibson, M. A. (1987). "Punjabi immigrants in an American high school." In G. Spindler & L. Spindler, (Eds.) Interpretive ethnography of education: At home and abroad (pp. 274- 281). Prospects Heights, Ill.: Waveland Press.

Gibson, M. A. (2002). The new Latino Diaspora and educational policy. In S. Wortham, E.G. Murillo, & E.T. Hamann (Eds). Education in the new Latino diaspora: Policy and the politics of identity (p. 243). Westport, CT. Ablex Publishing.

Giroux, H. (1992). Border crossings. New York: Routledge.

Giroux, H. (1996). Is there a place for cultural studies in colleges of education? In, H. A. Giroux, C. Landshear, P. McLaren, M. Peters (Eds.) Counternarratvies cultural studies and critical pedagogies in postmodern spaces (pp 41-58). New York: Routledge.

Glesne, C. (1997). That race feeling: Re-presenting research through poetic transcription. Qualitative Inquiry, 3(2), 202-222.

Golan, S., & Peterson, D. (2002). Promoting involvement of recent immigrant families in their chidlren's education. Cambridge, MA: Harvard Family Project. [Available at www.gse.harvard.edu/hfrp/projects/fine/resources/research/golan.html]

Gonzalez, J. (2001). A history of Latinos in America: Harvest of empire. New York: Penguin Books.

Goodman, A. (2003). Interview with Alan Goodman. In Race – The power of an illusion. California Newsreel. Retrieved 11/30/2004 from www.pbs.org/race/000_About/002_04- -background-02-01.htm

Gordon, E. (1997). Task force on the role and future of minorities. Educational Researcher, 26(3), 44-53.

Graves, J. Jr. (2003). Interview with Joshep Graves. In Race – The power of an illusion. California Newsreel. Retrieved 11/30/2004 from www.pbs.org/race/000_About/002_04- -background-02-01.htm

Guinier, L. & Torres, G. (2002). The miner's canary. Cambridge: Harvard University Press.

Gutmann, A. (1987). Democratic education. Princeton, NJ: Princeton University Press.

Hakuta, K. (1982). Mirror of language: The debate on bilingualism. New York: Basic Books, Inc.

Hammonds, E. (2003). Interview with Evelynn Hammonds. In Race – The power of an illusion. California Newsreel. Retrieved 11/30/2004 from www.pbs.org/race/000_About/002_04--background-02-01.htm

Harris, L. (Narrator), James, D. J. (Director). (2004). Episode 1: "The downward spiral" [Television series episode]. In J. D. James (Producer), Slavery and the making of America. New York: New York Broadcasting Company.

Harvard Family Research Project – Harvard Graduate School of Education Volume X Number 4 Winter 2004 – 2005. http://www.gse.harvard.edu/hfrp/content/eval/issue 28/winter2004-2005. pdf.

Hatch, T. (1998). How community action contributes to achievement. Educational Leadership, 55(8), 16-19.

Hayes-Bautista, D., Schink, W. O., & Chapa, J. (1988). The burden of support: Young Latinos in an aging society. Stanford, CA: Stanford University Press.

Heaney, T. (1995). Issues in Freirean pedagogy. http://www3.nl.edu/academics/cas/ace/resources/Documents/FreireIssues.cfm#Liberatory.

Henderson, A. (1987). The evidence continues to grow: Parent involvement improves student achievement. Columbia, MD: The National Committee for Citizens in Education.

Henry, M. (1996). Parent-school collaboration: Feminist organizational structures and school leadership. Albany: State University of New Press.

Hermes, M. (1999). Research methods as a situated response: Towards a first nations' methodology. In L. Parker, D. Deyhle, & S. Villenas (Eds.), Race is . . . race isn't: Critical race theory and qualitative studies in education (pp. 83-100). Boulder, CO: Westview Press.

Hidalgo, N. (1998). Toward a definition of a Latino family research paradigm. International Journal of Qualitative Studies in Education, 11, 103-120.

Hidalgo, N. (1999). Toward a definition of a Latino family research paradigm. In L. Parker, D. Deyhle, & S. Villenas (Eds.), Race is . . . race isn't: Critical race theory and qualitative studies in education (pp. 101-124). Boulder, CO: Westview Press.

Hodges, G. R., James, D. J. (Director). (2004). Episode 1: "The downward spiral" [Television series episode]. In J. D. James (Producer), Slavery and the making of America. New York: New York Broadcasting Company.

Horton, J. O. (Narrator), James, D. J. (Director). (2004). Episode 1: "The downward spiral" [Television series episode]. In J. D. James (Producer), Slavery and the making of America. New York: New York Broadcasting Company.

Horton, J. O. (2003). Interview with James O. Horton. In Race – The Power of an illusion. California Newsreel. Retrieved 11/30/2004 from http://www.pbs.org/race/000_About/002_04--background-02-01.htm

Howe, K. R. (1993). Equality of educational opportunity and the criterion of equal educational worth. Studies in Philosophy and Education 11: (pp. 329-337).

Howe, K. R. (1997). Understanding equal educational opportunity: Social justice, democracy and schooling. NY: Teachers College Press.

Jablonski, N. & Chaplin, G. (2002). In S. Iqbal. A new light on skin color. Online Extra, National Geographic Magazine, NGM Nov. 2002 S. http://magma.nationalgeo graphic.com/ngm/0211/feature2/online_extra.html

Jacobson, M. (2003). Episode Three: The difference between us. In Race – The Power of an illusion. California Newsreel. Retrieved 11/30/2004 from www.pbs.org/race/000_About/002_04--background-02-01.htm

Jay, M. (2003). Critical race theory, multicultural education, and the hidden curriculum of hegemony. Multicultural Perspectives An Official Journal of the National Association of Multicultural Education, 5(4), 3-9.

Jefferson, T. (1781). Notes on the State of Virginia. [Electronic version]. Paris: privately printed, 1782 [i.e. 1784]) 391 p.:map, tab.; octavo.

Jiménez, P. (2000). Immigration, assimilation, and the Mexican origin population. Field statement. Department of Sociology. Cambridge: Mass: Harvard University Press.

Jones, M. J. (1997). Prejudice and racism. New York: McGraw-Hill.

Jones-Correa, M. (1998). Commentary on immigration and public opinion. In M. Suárez-Orozco (ed.) in Crossings Mexican immigration in interdisciplinary perspectives (pp. 404-412). Cambridge, MA: Harvard University Press.

Kahlenberg, R. (2004/2005). Beyond Brown: The new wave of desegregation litigation. In F. Shultz (ed.), Multicultural education 2004/2005. Guilford, Connecticut: McGraw- Hill/Dushkin.

Kincheloe, J. L., & Steinberg, S. R. (1997). Changing multiculturalism. Buckingham, England: Open University press.

Krell, R. & Sherman, M. I. (1997). Genocide: A critical bibliographic review medical and psychological effects of concentration camps on holocaust survivors. (Eds.). New Brunswick: Transaction Publishers.

Kozol, J. (1991). Savage inequalities. New York: Basic Books.

Kozol, J. (2005). The shame of the nation the restoration of apartheid schooling in America. New York: Brown Publishers

Ladson-Billings, G. (1998) Preparing teachers for diverse student populations: a critical race theory perspective, Review of Research in Education, 24, 211-247.

Ladson-Billings, G. (1999). Just what is critical race theory and what's it doing in a nice field like education? In L. Parker, D. Deyhle, & S. Villenas (Eds), Race is . . . race isn't critical race theory and qualitative studies in education (pp. 7-30). Boulder: Westview Press.

Ladson-Billings, G. (2000). Racialized discourses and ethnic epistemologies, in: N. Denzin & Y. Lincoln (Eds) Handbook of qualitative research (Thousand Oaks, CA, Sage), 257-277.

Ladson-Billings, G., & Tate, W. (1995). Toward a critical race theory of education. Teachers College Record, 97 (1), 47-68.

Latino Eligibility Task Force. (1993). Latino student eligibility and participation in the University of California: Report number one of the Latino Eligibility Task Force. Santa Cruz, CA: University of California at Santa Cruz.

Lather, P. A., & Smitheis, C. (1997). Troubling the angels: Women living with HIV/AIDS. Boulder, CO. Westview Press.

Laureau, A. (1989). Home advantage. Social class and parent intervention in elementary education. London: Falmer Press.

Lareau, A. (2003). Unequal childhoods: Class, race, and family life. Berkeley: University of California Press.

LeCompte, M. D. & Schensul, J. J. (eds.) (1999). Designing and conducting ethnographic research. [Ethnographer's Toolkit, 1]. Walnut Creek, CA: Altamira Press.

Lewontin, R. (2003). Interview with Richard Lewontin. In Race – The Power of an illusion. California Newsreel. Retrieved 11/30/2004 from www.pbs.org/race/000_About/002_04- -background-02-01.htm

Lincoln, Y. S. & Guba, E. G. (1985). Naturalistic inquiry. Newbury Park, CA: Sage Publications.

Littlefield, D. C. (Narrator), James, D. J. (Director). (2004). Episode 1: "The downward spiral" [Television series episode]. In J. D. James (Producer), Slavery and the making of America. New York: New York Broadcasting Company.

López, G. R. (2001, Fall). The value of hard work: Lessons on parent involvement from an (im)migrant household. Harvard Educational Review, 71, 3, 416-437.

López, G. R. (2001, Fall). Effects of Latino parent involvement on academic achievement. Paper presented at the Annual Meeting of the American Education Research Association, Chicago, IL, March 24-28, 1997. 31 pages.

López, G. R. (2003). Parent involvement as racialized performance. In G. R. López & L. Parker (Eds), Interrogating racism in qualitative research methodology (pp. 71-95). New York: Peter Lang.

López, G. R. & Parker, P. (2003). Interrogating racism in qualitative research methodology. New York: Peter Lang.

Lopez, M. E. (1999).When discourses collide an ethnography of migrant children at home and in school. New York: Peter Lang Publishing, Inc.

MacDonald, V-M, Monkman, K. (2005). Setting the context: Historical perspectives on Latino/a Education. In P. Pedraza, & M. Rivera (Eds.), Latino education. Mahwah, New Jersey: Lawrence Erlbaum Inc.

Matute-Bianchi, M. E. (1986). Ethnic identities and patterns of school success and failure among Mexican-descent and Japanese-American students in a California high school: An ethnographic analysis." American Journal of Education 95, 23-55.

McIntosh, P. (1988). White privilege and male privilege: A personal account of coming to see correspondence through work in women's studies. Center for Research on Women. Working Paper Series No.189. Wellesley College, Wellesley, MA.

Mears, C. L. (2005). Esperiences of Columbine parents: Finding a way to tomorrow. (Unpublished doctoral dissertation, University of Denver). Dissertation Abstracts International, 66, 46.

Mears, C. L. (2005). *Experiences of Columbine parents: Finding a way to tomorrow.* Unpublished doctoral dissertation, University of Denver.

Mears, C. L. (2009). Interviewing for education and social science research: The gateway approach. New York: Palgrave Macmillan.

Méndez v. Westminster School District of Orange County, 64 F. Supp. 544 (D.C.CAL. 1946).

Miles, M. B. & Huberman, A. M. (1994). Qualitative data analysis: An expanded sourcebook. Thousand Oaks, CA: Sage.

Moles, O. C. (1993). Collaboration between schools and disadvantaged parents: Obstacles and openings. In N. F. Chavkin (Ed.), Families and schools in a pluralistic society (pp. 21- 49). Albany: State University of New York Press.

Montague, A. (1997). Man's most dangerous myth: The fallacy of race. Walnut Creek: CA. AltaMira Press.

Morgan, J. (Narrator), James, D. J. (Director). (2004). Episode 1: "The downward spiral" [Television series episode]. In J. D. James (Producer), Slavery and the making of America. New York: New York Broadcasting Company.Morris, V. G. &

Morris, G. M. & Morris, C. L. (2002). The price they paid. New York: Teachers College Press.

Morrison, T. (1997). Playing in the dark: Whiteness and the literary imagination. In R. Delgado & J. Stefancic, Critical white studies looking behind the mirror. Philadelphia: Temple University Press.

National Parent Teacher Association (2007). http://www.pta.org/spanish/index.asp.htm

Ngai, M. (2003). Episode Two: The story we tell. In Race – The Power of an illusion. California Newsreel. Retrieved 11/30/2004 from www.pbs.org/race/000_About/002 _04- -background-02-01.htm

Nieto, S. (1999). The light in their eyes: Creating multicultural learning communities. New York: Teachers College Press.

Nieto, S. (2004). Black, white, and us: The meaning of Brown v. Board of Education for Latinos. New York. Teachers College Press.

Noddings, N. (1992). The challenge to care in schools. New York: Teachers College Press.

Ogbu, J. (1987). Variability in minority school performance: A problem in search of an explanation. Anthropology and education quarterly 18:4 313-334.

Omi, M. & Winant, H. (1994). Racial formation in the United States from the 1960s to the 1990s. New York: Routhedge.

Orfield, G. (July, 1988). The growth and concentration of Hispanic enrollment and the future of American education. Paper presented at the annual conference of the National Council of La Raza, Albuquerque, NM.

Orfield, G. & Yun, J. T. (1999). Resegregation in American schools. Cambridge, MA: The Civil Rights Project, Harvard University.

Orfield, G. (2001). Schools more separate: Consequences of a decade of resegregation. Cambridge, MA: Civil Rights Project Harvard University.

Orfield, G. & Lee, C. (2005). Why segregation matters: Poverty and educational inequality. The Civil Rights Project Harvard University.

Olmedo, E. M. (2003) Accommodation and resistance: Latinas struggle for their children's education. Anthropology & Education Quarterly 34(4): 373-395.

Olson, S. (2001). The genetic archeology of race. In The Atlantic Monthly. April 2001.

Parea, J. F. (2000). The black/white binary paradigm of race. In R. Delgado & J. Stefancic (Eds.), Critical race theory the cutting edge (pp. 344-353). Philadelphia: Temple University Press.

Parker, L., Deyhle, D., Villenas, S. (1999). Race is . . . race isn': Critical race theory and qualitative studies in education. Boulder, CO: Westview Press.

Patton, M. Z. (1990). Qualitative evaluation and research methods (2nd ed.) Newbury Park, CA: Sage.

Pedraza, P., Rivera M. (2005). Latino education. Mahwah: New Jersey. Lawrence Erlbaum Associates, Inc.

Peters, M. & Lankshear, C. (1996). Postmodern counternarratives. In H. A. Giroux, C. Landshear, P. McLaren, M. Peters (Eds.), Counternarratives cultural studies and critical pedagogies in postmodern spaces. (pp. 1-39). New York: Routledge Press.

Pew Hispanic Research Center (2005). Trends in 200. Hispanics people in motion. Washington, DC.

Pizarro, M. (1999). Adelante: Toward social justice and empowerment in Chicana/o communities and Chicana/o studies. In L. Parker, D. Deyhle, & S. Villenas (Eds.), Race is . . . race isn't: Critical race theory and qualitative studies in education (pp. 53-81). Boulder, CO: Westview Press.

Plessy v. Ferguson, 163 U.S. 537 (1896)

Plyer v. Doe, 457 U.S. 202 (1982)

Pritchard, J. (2004, March). A Mexican worker dies each day. Daily News Associated Press. Retrieved March 14, 2004, from http://customwire.ap.org/dynamic/stories /D/DYING TOWORK?SITE=CAWOOD&SECT

Rawls, J. (1971). A theory of justice. Cambridge: Harvard University Press.

Richarson, L. (202). Poetic representations of interviews. In J. F. Gubrium & J. A. Holstein (Eds.), Handbook of interview research: Context and method pp.877-891). Thousand Oaks, CA: Sage.

Robledo, M. (1989). The answer: Valuing youth in school and families. San Antonio, TX: Intercultural Development Research Association.

Rose, M. (1989). Lives on the boundary. New York: The Free Press.

Schensul S. Schensul, J. J. & LeCompte M. D. (1999). Essential ethnographic methods observations, interviews, and questionnaires. [Ethnographer's Toolkit, 2]. Walnut Creek, CA: Altamira Press.

Scribner, J.D., Young, M.D., & Pedroza, A. (1999). Building collaborative relationships with parents. In P. Reyes, J.D. Scribner, & A.P. Scribner (Eds.), Lessons from high-performing Hispanic schools: Creating learning communities. New York: Teachers College Press.

Selden, S. (1999). Inheriting shame: The story of eugenics and racism in America. New York: Teachers College, Columbia University

Seller, M. & Weis, L. (1997). Beyond black and white. (Eds.) Albany: State University of New York Pres.

Simon, R. (1994). Forms of insurgency in the production of popular memories: The Columbus quincentenary and the pedagogy of countercommemoration. In H. Giroux and P. McLaren (Eds.), Between borders pedagogy and the politics of cultural studies. New York: Routledge.

Sipes, D. S. B. (1993). Cultural values and American-Indian families. In N. F. Chavkin (Ed.), Families and schools in a pluralistic society (pp. 157-174). Albany: State University of New York Press.

Sleeter, C.E., & Grant, C.A. (1987). An analysis of multicultural education in the United States. Harvard Educational Review, 57(40, 441-444.

Sleeter, C. E. & Grant, C. A. (2003). Making choices for multicultural education: Five approaches to race, class, and gender. New York: John Wiley & Sons.

Sleeter, C. E. & Bernal, D. D., (2004). Critical pedagogy, critical race theory, and antiracist education implications for multicultural education. In J. A. Banks & C. A. .McGee Banks (Eds). Handbook of research on multicultural education (pp. 240-258). San Francisco: John Wiley & Sons, Inc.

Smedley, A. (1999). Race in North America: Origin and evolution of a worldview. Boulder: Westview Press.

Smith, G. P. (2004). Desegregation and resegregation after Brown; implications for multicultural teacher education. Multicultural Perspectives National Association for Multicultural Education 6, 2004 26-32

Solorzano, D. G. (1997). Images and words that words that wound: critical race theory, racial stereotyping and teacher education, Teacher Educaiton Quarterly, 24, 5-19.

Solorzano, D. G. (1998). Critical race theory, race, and gender microagrressions, and the experience of Chicana and Chicano scholars. International Journal of Qualitative Studies in Education, 11, 121-136.

Sosa, A. S. (1997). Involving Hispanic parents in educational activities through collaborative relationships. Bilingual Research Journal, 21, (2), 1-8.

Spradley, J. (1980). Participant observation. Belmont, CA: Thomson Learning, Inc.

Spring, J. (2001). The American school: 1642-2000. New York: McGraw-Hill.

Suarez-Orozco, M. (1989). Central American refugees and U.S. high schools: A psychosocial study of motivational achievement. Stanford, California: Stanford University Press.

Suarez-Orozco, M. M. & Suarez-Orozco, C. M. (1993). The cultural psychology of Hispanic immigrants: Implications for educational research. In P. Phelan & A. L. Davidson, (Eds.). Renegotiating cultural diversity in American schools (pp. 108-138). New York: Teachers College Press.

Suárez-Orozco M. M. and Páez M. M. (2002). Latinos remaking America. Los Angeles: University of California Press.

Suárez-Orozco, C. (2001). Afterword: Understanding and serving the children of immigrants. Harvard Educational Review. 71 579-589 pp.

Suárez-Orozco C., Suárez-Orozco M. & Doucet F. (2004). The academic engagement and achievement of Latino Youth. In Banks, J. A & Banks, C.A.M, Handbook of research on multicultural education (420-437). San Francisco: Jossey-Bass.

Tillman, L. (2002). Culturally sensitive research approaches: An African American perspective. Educational Researcher. 31 (9), 3-12.

Tinkler, B. (2002). A review of literature on Hispanic/Latino parent involvement in K12 education. Research Report, University of Denver: Assets for Colorado Youth.

Tonso, K. L. & Colombo, M. (2006). Parental choice, educational opportunity, and the decision to decharter an urban, black, middle school. Journal of School Choice, 1(1), 43 pp.

U.S. Bureau of the Census. (1992). Statistical Abstract of the United States 1992. Washington, DC: U.S. Government Printing Office.

U.S. Census Bureau Census 2000, Summary File 1. Hispanic Population by Type for Regions, States, and Puerto Rico 1990 & 2000. Washington, DC.

U.S. Census Bureau 2000. Decennial Census data and Census. Supplementary Survey (C2SS).

U.S. Census Bureau (2001a). The Hispanic Population. Washington, DC: Internet release date, March 2001.

U.S. Census Bureau (2001b). Overview of race and Hispanic origin. Washington, DC: Internet release date, May 2001.

U.S. Census Bureau. Current Population Survey (March 1999). Ethnic and Hispanic Statistics Branch, Population Division. Washington, DC: Internet release date, March 2001.

Vaca, N. (2004). The presumed alliance. New York: HarperCollins Publishers.

Valdés, F. Culp J. & Harris, A. (2002). Crossroads, directions, and a new critical race theory. Philadelphia: Temple University Press

Valdés, F. (2004). LatCrit theory, praxis, and community: A conceptual overview www. latcrit.org.

Valdés, V. (1996). Con respeto. New York: Teachers College Press

Valencia, R. (R. (1991). Chicano school failure and success: Research and policy agendas for the 1990s. New York: Falmer Press.

Van Maanen, J. (1988). Tales of the field. Chicago: The University of Chicago Press.

Villanueva, I. (1997). The voices of Chicano families: Life stories, maintaining bilingualism, and cultural awareness. In M. Seller and L. Weis (Eds.), Beyond black and white new faces and voices in U.S. schools (pp 61-79). New York: State University of New York Press.

Villenas, S. (1996). The colonizer/colonized Chicana ethnographer: Identity, marginalization, and co-option in the field. Harvard Educational Review, 66(4), 711- 731.

Villenas, S. & Deyhle, D. (1999). Critical race theory and ethnographies challenging the stereotypes: Latino families, schooling resilience and resistance. Curriculum Inquiry 29 413-445.

Wade, P. (1997). Race and ethnicity in Latin America. Sterling: Pluto Press.

Willis, P. (1977). Learning to labor. New York: Columbia University Press.

Willis, P. (2000). The ethnographic imagination. Malden: MS Blackwell Publishers Inc.

Wolcott, H. F. (2001). Writing up qualitative research. Thousand Oaks, CA: Sage Publications, Inc.

Wong-Fillmore, L. 1991. "When learning a second language means losing the first. Early Childhood Research Quarterly, 6, 323-346.

Wood, P. (Narrator), James, D. J. (Director). (2004). The downward spiral. [Television series episode]. In J. D. James (Producer), Slavery and the making of America. New York: New York Broadcasting Company.

Woodson, C. G. (1977). The miseducation of the Negro. New York: AMS Press. (Original work published 1933).

Yosso, T. J. (2005). Whose culture has capital? A critical race theory discussion of community cultural wealth. Race Ethnicity Education, 8(1), 69-91.

Young, I. M. (1990). Justice and the politics of difference. Princeton, NJ: Princeton University Press.

Zinn, H. (1999). A people's history of the United States: 1492 – present. New York: Harper Collins Publishers Inc.

BIOGRAPHICAL NOTE

Jorge Dante-Hernández Prósperi was born in Argentina in 1944. He is a retired educator who for 45 years served as a Public and Independent School Spanish High School IB/AP Instructor, Middle School Principal, Admissions Director and college adjunct to the School of Education and Center for Latino/a and Latin American Studies (Wayne State University), Harvard Principal Center Summer Institute 1988 and PhD in Curriculum and Instruction from Wayne State University with emphasis on Diversity Literacy as it applies to Critical Theories, Social Constructs and Agencies.

~

. . . Amé, fui amado, el sol acarició mi faz.
¡Vida, nada me debes! ¡Vida, estamos en paz!

. . . I loved, I was loved, the sun caressed my face.
Life, you owe me nothing! Life, we are at peace!

En Paz - Amado Nervo - 1915

Printed in the United States
By Bookmasters